DIG DEEP IN ONE PLACE

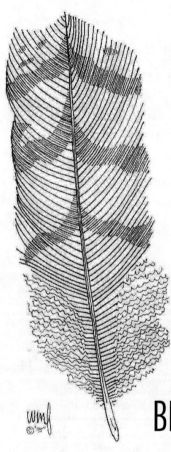

DIG DEEP IN ONE PLACE

A Couple's Journey to a Spiritual Life

BILL AND SANDY FIFIELD

BALBOA
PRESS
A DIVISION OF HAY HOUSE

Copyright © 2011 Bill and Sandy Fifield

All rights reserved. No part of this book may be used or reproduced by any means, graphic, electronic, or mechanical, including photocopying, recording, taping or by any information storage retrieval system without the written permission of the publisher except in the case of brief quotations embodied in critical articles and reviews.

Balboa Press books may be ordered through booksellers or by contacting:

Balboa Press
A Division of Hay House
1663 Liberty Drive
Bloomington, IN 47403
www.balboapress.com
1-(877) 407-4847

Because of the dynamic nature of the Internet, any web addresses or links contained in this book may have changed since publication and may no longer be valid. The views expressed in this work are solely those of the author and do not necessarily reflect the views of the publisher, and the publisher hereby disclaims any responsibility for them.

The author of this book does not dispense medical advice or prescribe the use of any technique as a form of treatment for physical, emotional, or medical problems without the advice of a physician, either directly or indirectly. The intent of the author is only to offer information of a general nature to help you in your quest for emotional and spiritual well-being. In the event you use any of the information in this book for yourself, which is your constitutional right, the author and the publisher assume no responsibility for your actions.

Any people depicted in stock imagery provided by Thinkstock are models, and such images are being used for illustrative purposes only. Certain stock imagery © Thinkstock.

ISBN: 978-1-4525-3884-6 (e)
ISBN: 978-1-4525-3885-3 (sc)
ISBN: 978-1-4525-3883-9 (hc)

Library of Congress Control Number: 2011916704

Printed in the United States of America

Balboa Press rev. date: 10/05/2011

For Pamela, who was there with her compassion, experience, strength, honesty, and humor when we were ready to start this incredible adventure. Thank you for a real recipe to give this away.

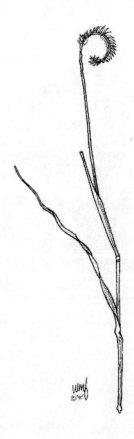

Bill and Sandy, 1968

"To find water, you do not dig small pits all over the place but drill deep in one place only."
—Sri Nisargadatta Maharaja

Photo credit—William Thach Studios, Denver CO

CONTENTS

ILLUSTRATIONS by Bill Fifield xi

Foreword xiii

Preface xv

Introduction xvii

PART ONE
WHAT IT WAS LIKE 1

Chapter One
Point of No Return 3

Chapter Two
Childhood Memories—Bill 13

Chapter Three
Air Force Brat—Sandy 21

Chapter Four
Our Life Together 29

PART TWO
WHAT HAPPENED 41

Chapter Five
Arrival at the Temple, Bill—July 28, 1992, 6:05 p.m. 43

Chapter Six
Resistance—Sandy 51

Chapter Seven
Let's Start Digging, Bill—Steps 1-6 61

Chapter Eight
Discovery of Denial, Sandy—Steps 1-6 69

Chapter Nine
What Can I Bring?, Bill—Steps 7-12 83

Chapter Ten
Faith is Action, Sandy—Steps 7-12... 93

PART THREE

WHAT IT'S LIKE NOW 105

Chapter Eleven
   Let's Dig Deeper—The Twelve Traditions 107
Chapter Twelve
   Twelve Concepts of World Service 119
Chapter Thirteen
   Love, Light, and Joy—Recovery and Art................................. 131
Chapter Fourteen
   Passing it On—The Circle of Recovery 143

Afterword... 159
Gratitude 161
Resources... 163
Author Bio 167

ILLUSTRATIONS BY BILL FIFIELD

The illustrations in this book are a direct result of the spiritual awakening I had in my second week at Harmony Foundation. The way feathers look suddenly became crystal clear. Their complex simplicity flowed through my arm with no effort at all. The endless beauty of the world seemed sharply focused. When the infinite varieties of grasses caught my attention, the same thing happened.

Creativity is like sitting in God's pocket and is the birth of inspiration and intuition. I am grateful, and I stand in awe of the amazing number of gifts that fill my life. Thank you.

Cover photo by Sandy Fifield

FOREWORD

In a lifetime, if we are lucky, we may have the opportunity to study with a true master. I am one of the fortunate ones, for I have been given the gift to study with two.

The first thing I noticed about Bill Fifield was his piercing blue eyes. Filling the room with his presence, he greeted me with a bellowing laugh, planted a kiss on my cheek, and enthusiastically patted my back with the kind of greeting that almost left a mark. This was our first hello. *Just who is this man?* I wondered. He certainly stood out from the crowd! He had that certain something—a *je ne sai quoi*, as the French say. And I did *not* know what it was. I never guessed that he was to become one of the most important people in my life.

Then, three years later, I had the opportunity to meet his wife. Sandy had a softer presence with eyes that burned as brightly as Bill's and beauty that radiated from within. Her grace was what struck me, leaving a mark on my heart. These people had something that I wanted; I had met my teachers

And so the journey began. Weekly meetings and daily calls with the Fifields became a foundation of my spiritual program. Day after day, I called and was met with love on the other end of the line. This was the kind of love that saves lives; the kind of love that doesn't listen to excuses, doesn't hear sob stories, doesn't feel pity; the kind of love that knows who you are when you forget; and the kind of love you can count on. Week after week, I would sit across the table from one of them and bathe in their wisdom. Sometimes I would scribble madly, hoping to capture every word they said; other times I would listen openly, trusting that my heart heard what it needed to hear and knowing that I could always ask to be reminded again.

During my years of study with the Fifields, I deepened my spiritual path to a level I had only previously hoped for. I moved through life-changing events with grace I didn't know I had. Their messages of compassion echoed through my head when I found myself fuming with impatience in a long line or overreacting to a hapless driver cutting me off in traffic. "Be the gift, be the gift, be the gift. See what you can bring," was the mantra. Then, in equally important moments, when I was feeling sorry for myself, I would remember that the most effective and valuable action I could take was to get out of myself and help someone else. I also experienced the humility to allow others their own path versus my typical desire to control an outcome. Utilizing many metaphors for the human tendency to succumb to fear, they likened fear to a tiny insect with a microphone shouting from the corner of a room. If I believed what it said, I would grant it the power to become a brutal, smoke-breathing dragon that would kill me if I let it. "Stop gathering evidence for the lie!" they would exclaim, seemingly in unison. They also provided a rallying cry of an affirmation: "I stand at the portals of creation. I am ready to receive." This remains in smeary chalk on my refrigerator to remind me of what is possible. As they guided, supported, and loved me into being who I am supposed to be, they also continually pointed out that I am the only one who is holding me back.

All of this would be impressive even if I was the only one who benefited from their wisdom. Instead, as they listened to my pain, upset, errors, and defects, as well as my joy, success, and glory, they were also listening to the tales of hundreds of others. The phone never stopped ringing, and the knocks on the door never ceased to echo. And they continuously greeted it all with a hearty hello and a commitment to be of service. Unlike most people, the Fifields know why they are here. With clarity of purpose, they graciously greet those who suffer yet are willing to grow beyond the pain. Bill and Sandy have the gift to help others, and they pass it on with love.

My wish for you is that you accept the gift that is being offered to you through this book. You may not be blessed with the opportunity to sit across the table from the Fifields. Therefore, I suggest you fasten your seatbelt. Open yourself to what you are about to read; soak it up and let it speak to your heart. Allow it to challenge you and guide you as you move forward on your journey. Then, as Bill and Sandy always say, go out in the world and *be* that gift.

Kristen Moeller, MS
Author of *Waiting for Jack*

PREFACE

We did not write *Dig Deep in One Place* as a substitute for the Twelve Steps, for attending fellowship meetings, or for getting a sponsor to assist in understanding the spiritual principles or service work. This is not Alcoholics Anonymous. We did write this book as a supplement to your understanding of the Twelve Steps, much like listening to a speaker meeting.

This book begins with the last eight months of our denial, delusion, and insanity and continues with our separate childhood memories. We then combine our stories for our early life together. We separate again for our experiences as we worked the Twelve Steps, and we will reconnect for a discussion of the Traditions and Concepts of Twelve-Step fellowships.

We then share our memories of the incredible journey of the last nineteen years as we have learned more about the spiritual principles and practicing a spiritual life. We continue with a discussion of how art completes the circle of unity, recovery, and service as we stand at the portals of creation, finally ready to receive.

In conclusion we have the stories of seven people whose lives have been changed by their experience with the Twelve Steps.

INTRODUCTION

"How quickly I accuse, condemn, sentence and execute. Why do I begin with you and not myself?"

—Sri Nisargadatta Maharaj

We have been successful artists and teachers since 1970. Our artistic collaboration of "fifields, THE STUDIO" has produced over forty years worth of "one of a kind, one at a time" pieces of art. When unconscious selfishness and addiction brought all of this to a halt, our self-imposed crisis could no longer be ignored. We were forced beyond the narrow view of our indulgence. We found relief in the Twelve Steps. This is the story of that spiritual awakening. With it came renewed enthusiasm and understanding of the meaning of life and art. As a result, our art has blossomed, and service to others has become our focus. A spiritual life is service to others. Our goal is to open a door to spirituality for anyone using the Twelve Steps and clearly explain the results of doing them. *Dig Deep in One Place* does just that from actual experience. There is no theory and no opinion. It's not a cult or religion; it's about waking up. It's about spirituality.

Dig Deep in One Place is aimed at anyone who has ever used the Twelve Steps for recovery or anyone else who has ever been curious about the process of the Twelve Steps.

There are over 250 mutual help groups using the Twelve Steps as a practical method for recovery from any type of obsessive-compulsive behavior, such as alcoholism and drug addiction, overeating or under eating, or working too much. There is even an Artist's (ARTS) Anonymous to deal with the fear of creating art. This can encompass all phases of the spiritual disease of fear, which afflicts all humans and is manifested in hundreds of different ways.

This book is in the format of a Twelve-Step fellowship "speaker meeting" where an individual tells his or her story using a format of:

"What it was like, what happened, and what it's like now." These meetings usually last from one to one and a half hours. The book obviously contains much more detail than a one-hour talk can contain. It narrates the simultaneous stories of a couple who have stayed together for over forty-five years through addiction, alcoholism, and co-dependence to come to a spiritual life of happy, joyous freedom.

It is not our intent to tell anyone how to do this or give specific instructions on how to work the Twelve Steps but to present our experience in the desire that it will bring hope and strength to the reader. This is the traditional means of communication among members of Twelve-Step fellowships of any kind addressing the myriad of difficulties that the human mind can dream up.

Without exception, identification with any specific Twelve-Step group at the level of the media violates the spirit of Tradition Eleven. To speak generally about the Twelve Steps and recovery is the personal choice we have made in writing this book.

We each had our ideas about life. We looked on the various situations in that life together in totally different ways, and yet we stayed together to come to recovery. True to form, we approached the Twelve Steps in our own unique ways to come to the same conclusion: that the Steps are a practical way to deal with the spiritual disease of fear no matter how it is manifested. It could manifest through food, sex, alcohol, drugs, gambling, bitterness, trauma, anger, stress, anxiety, or depression. Any one of these things is potentially life threatening. At the very least, they can make our lives and the lives of those around us miserable.

Our descent into addiction was not accompanied by great drama or tragedy. We were each brought up in good families who taught us right from wrong, who were loving and supportive, and who stayed married and were loyal to their spouses. The questions are: Why did each of us take such a long time to grow up, to take responsibility and learn to help others? Why were we so selfish and self-centered that we each believed with all our hearts that we deserved to get something for nothing? What were the methods we used to deal with the pervasive fear in our lives?

This is the story of that journey to a crisis in our lives that we could not ignore, postpone, or evade. It became life or death in a very literal way. It is the story of how that selfishness and laziness affected our families, and it's the story of the discovery of a way out of that place of despair. But more importantly, it is the story of a very practical way out of that pit. The Twelve Steps gave us that way. The Twelve Steps are literally a practical set of actions to change your life.

Our passion is the Twelve Steps. We never knew there were directions before. It seemed like everyone knew what to do but us, that we were out of the room when the life instructions were given out. Turns out we were not alone in this thinking. Every day we see people run over by their lives just like we were. We now have a way to be of real help. It is the most fulfilling thing we have ever done. Our enthusiasm has never wavered to see people have a spiritual awakening. To watch them help others makes us rich beyond measure. We have never met anyone who would not benefit from this truly simple and practical program. For nineteen years we have been changing the world one person at a time. We have done this over twelve hundred times. Imagine having a larger audience. Imagine presenting this gift to tens of thousands of people. By showing others how to help someone else with this ridiculously simple and easy recipe, the whole universe could change. Being relieved of the bondage of fear automatically releases the passion. The word gratitude does not begin to express how thankful we are to be able to pass this on.

PART ONE

What It Was Like

"Remember, this is the great adventure!"
—Sandy

CHAPTER ONE

Point of No Return

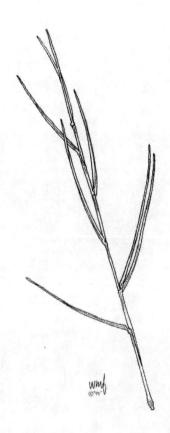

"More is not enough."
—Bill

July 28, 1992

Bill weighed 285 pounds when we dropped him off at Harmony Foundation treatment center. He was bright red and sweating like a butcher. His kidneys were shutting down, and his liver was protruding out his side. His blood pressure set a world record, and even with no signs of intoxication, he blew a .045, drunk by anyone's standard.

So how did it ever come to this? Going back in time to Christmas 1991, we can trace the final steps to this inevitable conclusion. We were not invited to the traditional Christmas get-together with Sandy's family; instead we were invited to dinner with Sandy's mother and stepfather—just the four of us in a public place, a nice restaurant. We were baffled, but we went anyway; we wanted and needed the gifts that would be given. We brought presents too. In our complete delusion and denial, we had decided to give portraits of ourselves to our friends and family. Although we couldn't see the truth at the time, this portrait was terrifying. Bill had gained weight despite, or maybe because of, the blood pressure meds he was on. He looked like he might just burst if pricked with a pin. Sandy looked baffled and scared. Neither of us had light in our eyes, but we thought we looked great! We made every effort to appear and act normal, and managed to escape the scene with the gifts and without having offended anyone too badly, but even we were starting to sense that there was something very wrong.

After Bill's birthday on January 11, the "holidays" were officially over, and we could get back to normal. Well, our normal anyway. We continued to try to prove that all was okay in our house. In February, we bought a 1985, new to us, Subaru wagon. As we drove to Denver in Bill's old International Scout to pick it up, it got later and later, and soon it was completely dark. Sandy drove the new Subaru, and Bill was to follow in the Scout. What a terrifying drive for both of us. We had both been drinking all day. Bill's night vision was nonexistent as he stared out into a wall of headlights that stretched across the windshield. Sandy couldn't find the lights, heater, defroster, or windshield wipers in the new car in the dark. It was dangerous for us and all those around us. Still, we were okay! Everything was fine! We had just bought a new car.

Early in April 1992, an old friend from Minnesota called Sandy's mother to say, "Bill has been calling me during his blackouts. Something has to be done about his drinking, or he will kill himself or someone else very soon." This friend had been sober for five years. During a conversation to plan a family wedding that was taking place in Telluride, Colorado, in late June, Sandy's mother confronted her with this information, asking, "What is really going on with Bill and you? Is everything okay in your house? Can we trust him to behave at the wedding festivities? Do we need to stage an intervention?" Sandy broke down and told the truth. She said, "Yes, we need to have an intervention, but not until after the wedding." Now there were two events being planned for that summer—one just as much a beginning as the other, as it turned out.

Now, how did Sandy behave with this secret information? She had to withdraw from attempt to control battle with Bill that she had been engaging in prior to this decision. That behavior included constantly asking, "Have you been drinking? How much?" She had to control her own drinking, lest she tell the secret about the intervention to take place three weeks after the wedding (July 28). She still drank with Bill, but he was vaguely aware that something had changed. He would look at her and inquire, "What's going on?" It was extremely difficult for Sandy to keep the secret. There was still the wish that it really wouldn't be necessary to have an intervention, that everything would somehow magically get better on its own. Sandy continued to plan for both events.

We decided a camping trip to the Utah desert would be fun before the wedding. We would make it a full week of celebration, including the wedding. As it turned out, it was our last hurrah with drugs and alcohol.

The first full day started with drinks all around as we packed the Subaru in the rain. That summer, we needed to go to the desert to have any summer at all. We argued and drank all the way to Grand Junction, Colorado. We arrived drunk, tired, and hungry, found a motel, and ventured out for some food. The first restaurant was so busy that, after an hour and more drinks, it became obvious that our food order had been lost, so we left. After threatening an employee at the next restaurant, we decided to return to the motel to eat some of our camping food and drink the rest of the vodka and rum we had brought. We finally passed out after an emotional and hurtful argument. In the morning, filled with fresh resolve to have a great time, we replenished our booze and beer supply and were on our way to Utah, where we planned to camp along the Colorado River near Moab.

Drinking beer all the way, we finally found a campsite that was located deep in the tamarisk and high above the river. The only access to the river was down a twenty-five-foot mudslide. The tamarisk was dark and creepy, and there were spiders and bugs all around. We didn't like it, but again we were drunk, tired, hot, irritable, and hungry, so we had to set up camp fast. After a quick meal, many more cocktails, and a loud argument that echoed off the canyon walls, we passed out in the tent with the agreement that we would buy no more alcohol the next day. We were sure that we could make do with the supply we had left.

Awakening with vicious hangovers, we found a new campsite on an open bend of the Colorado River, a beautiful spot. We pitched our tent under a small tree where we could see the river flowing. There was an easy-to-get-to small, sandy beach. We spent the day setting up camp, drinking, swimming, and sunbathing. By early afternoon, we were out of booze, even the beer, and we were starting to feel the effects of withdrawal from alcohol and dehydration. Bill was shaking and sweating a dry sweat, and neither of us felt well. We vaguely sensed that this was more than just another hangover.

We somehow made it through an extremely strange and long, hot night. After a violent windstorm that sounded like a freight train coming down the canyon, slammed into our tent, and nearly rolled us into the river, a large group of young campers arrived after midnight to set up camp next to us. We were jolted awake to lots of noise and activity. We, of course, thought we were about to be attacked. In the morning, we broke camp in a hurry to get to Moab and find the liquor store, a difficult thing to do in Utah.

We restocked with beer, vodka, and rum, and off we went to the grocery store for ice, dry ice, mixers, and some food. For our next night, we decided to visit Arches National Park and then camp at Dead Horse Point State Park. Dead Horse Point was a natural spot to corral and catch wild horses in the 1800s, but some horses had been left by mistake to die of thirst. We felt about the same way even though there was a gorgeous view of a horseshoe bend in the Colorado River. We looked longingly down at the river far below and thought, *The Subaru has four-wheel drive, and the map shows a four-wheel drive road leading to the river from here. Let's go!* We pass a large sign warning, "POINT OF NO RETURN, CHECK BRAKES HERE." Sandy tapped the brakes, and off we went, straight down the side of the mesa. The only other vehicles we saw were huge, high, four-wheel drive Jeep touring cars whose occupants all looked at us like we were crazy, and well, we were. Three hours later, we reached the river bottom. The car was overheating and pushed to its limits, and so were we.

After checking out several potential campsites, we found a private one close to the river, but it was in the tamarisk and a mess. We sat in the river with fresh drinks to cool off. Then we worked to set up camp and cook some dinner. As the sun went down, the air was suddenly filled with mosquitoes. Our only defense was to head for the tent with dinner and all our booze to wait out the night. We drank until we passed out to the hum of predatory insects bouncing off the tent all night. Just the thought of leaving our refuge for any reason was terrifying.

With sunrise, the mosquitoes were gone, so we packed up and headed to Telluride for the wedding. First we stopped in Moab for more vodka, rum, and beer. We had promised to be on our best behavior for the wedding events, so we stashed the vodka and rum in the Subaru and promised each other that we would not touch it until after the wedding festivities. Beer and wine were approved, and there were plenty of opportunities to drink those without being noticed.

Arriving in Telluride in late afternoon, we had a lovely room provided for us at the New Sheridan Hotel that looked out on the main street of downtown Telluride. Bill immediately disappeared into the bar for a couple of shots of vodka. The rest of the family was already there and checked in, so after a quick shower and a change from camping grubbies to resort clothes, we went to dinner with the whole family. Since no one was really paying attention to us, we were able to sneak enough extra wine to maintain our blood alcohol level, but not appear drunk.

The next day, Saturday, the wedding day finally arrived. The event was to take place on Hastings Mesa northwest of Telluride. It was a beautiful mountain property complete with wildflowers in profusion, plenty of aspen trees, and lots of beer and wine. With old friends and new, both of us behaved nicely, with no problems. We even got away with snorting some cocaine someone had brought. The beautiful afternoon wound down, and we were off to Ouray, Colorado, where the tab had been picked up again at the Beaumont Hotel for the family. We had another dinner with lots of wine, and we were off to bed. It was an old hotel with paper-thin walls and transom windows above the doors. The night started off peacefully, but soon the tranquility was broken by snoring—Bill's snoring. Some said it sounded like a bull elephant in rut, extremely loud. Sandy didn't hear a thing. She had learned long ago that if she passed out before it started, she could sleep through the din, but everyone else in the hotel gathered outside the door to marvel at the sheer volume of noise coming from our room. We guess that the family and other guests must have gotten some sleep because they didn't drag us out of the room and murder us. We all met for brunch Sunday morning, with plenty of Bloody Marysfor everyone. We endured some kidding because of the snoring, and then we were free from the family at last.

Now the real reason we had stashed the vodka and rum became clear; alcohol sales were illegal on Sunday in Colorado in 1992. We congratulated ourselves on our foresight and drove off to the Orvis Hot

Springs in Ridgeway, Colorado, where we planned to spend the night, soak in the clothing-optional hot springs, and drink all afternoon. The results were predictable: another endless argument, and we eventually passed out to wake in the morning and drive home to Conifer.

Sandy was back to work the next day thinking, *Well, everything went great. Maybe we don't need to have an intervention after all. Bill did behave at the wedding. It almost seemed like the good old days.* But there he was when she arrived home, passed out drunk on the couch, dead to the world. It continued to get worse instead of better. Plans for the intervention progressed.

Intervention day arrived. Bill had been told that we were invited to a "party" hosted by our friend from Minnesota starting at 4:00 p.m. at a small cabin in Allen's Park, just south of Estes Park, Colorado. We started out early at 10:00 a.m. We were both nervous for different reasons. Bill was anxious to get to the "party" so he could drink openly, and Sandy had to figure out how to stall until 4:00. We couldn't get to the "party" before the appointed time. After stopping at liquor stores in Conifer and Evergreen, Sandy decided that she just had to stop at a casino in Blackhawk to gamble for a while to kill some time. The drinks we ordered tasted like water and had absolutely no effect on either of us. We fed the slot machines for a couple of hours and finally started again for Allen's Park. Because the drinks at the casino had no effect, we had to stop again in Nederland to buy just a little more booze for the "party."

The directions to the cabin were confusing, especially since Bill was looking for lots of cars indicating a party, but all the participants of the intervention had hidden their cars. Bill was getting suspicious, asking, "Where's the party?" again and again. Just then our friend from Minnesota strolled out of the woods wearing an outrageous ten-gallon Stetson hat with feathers all over it. He said, "Come on in the cabin." We stepped into the front room, and there sat the only six people left in our life who would still talk to us and one total stranger.

The stranger opened his mouth and said the words that would change our lives forever. Looking directly at Bill, he said, "We know what's been going on. These family and friends are scared to death that you are about to kill yourself or somebody else with your drinking."

He continued, "They want to know if you would be willing to go into treatment today for addiction."

Bill opened his mouth, and out came, "Okay." There was a stunned silence.

One of the participants jumped to his feet and said, "Now wait just a minute, we have been terrified of this moment for months. We have written letters to try to talk you into going into treatment, so you're going to sit there and listen to them."

There we sat for over an hour while they read their letters of love and concern. Bill still agreed to go to Harmony, but he was starting to shake and sweat. The stranger asked if he wanted another drink before we drove to the treatment center in Estes Park. Bill said, "No, I'm done."

CHAPTER TWO

Childhood Memories—Bill

"You can't get into heaven carrying a bag of garbage."
—Bill

I don't know why I got to spend so much time with my grandparents as a kid. Maybe my folks were having some kind of difficulties, but I just loved it. First I spent time with them out on the farm and then in the tiny town of Fountain, Minnesota, where Grandpa retired after he gave his farm to the boys (my uncles). I loved helping Grandma pick corn and raspberries in her outrageous garden, cooking loose meat hamburgers, and the very special way she fixed the corn. I have never tasted anything like it anywhere. She would cup my face in her hands, smile, and call me Billy.

I remember fishing with Grandpa, sitting on the banks of the Zumbro River, using bamboo poles and red and white bobbers. I never seemed to catch anything and there was not much talk, but I remember being surrounded by his love and caring. It was the same parked in rocking chairs on his tiny porch greeting passersby. You could tell who did or didn't interest him by his turning his pocket model hearing aid up or down. It sounded like feedback from a rock star's guitar. I remember going to the post office with him. When he retired, he bought a brand-new baby blue Chevy pickup. Now, the post office was only on the far side of the adjacent block. Don't forget, he was deaf, so we would peel out of the driveway, spitting gravel everywhere up to the stop sign on the corner. With me hanging on for dear life, we burned rubber around the corner to the right; one more right, and there was the post office. There were always a few of Grandpa's cronies there. He would always introduce me and make sure I was included. Then we would repeat the performance back to the house. It's a sweet, sweet memory.

I always meant to go back home and tell Grandpa how much I loved him, but what I got to do was go back and carry his coffin. It broke my heart. It took years to forgive myself. So years later when Grandma was living with my folks and Mom called saying she wanted to see me, I responded at once. We sat together while she embroidered a dishcloth for me. She had pro wrestling on the TV because she thought that's what boys liked to do on weekends. "Uff da and my, my Billy," she said while patting my hand. What an awesome woman. She seemed to have been born brimming with spiritual principles. Her whole life was filled with giving. There is no telling how many babies got booties and blankets and how many folks she kept from going hungry. Three days after we got home to Colorado, she died. Thank you, God, that I got to tell her I loved her and how much she meant to me.

What happened to that little boy so full of joy running through the alfalfa with his wooden sword chasing butterflies, the little boy staring in wonder at the garden spiders' webs strung between two milk weeds and glinting with dew? It was just my little dog, Chub, a white-and-brown potpourri of terriers, and me. He was the bravest companion in the world. I remember a fat, wobbly skunk staggering out of the woods headed straight for my mother. Chub shot off the porch and started harassing its flanks. Foam was flying from the skunk's mouth as it tried to shake that blur of nips and snarls. My dad finally dispatched it with a blow from a shovel and took it to our vet to confirm it had rabies. That little doggie was something. He saved me from attacks by the vicious Leghorn roosters and from a very large, mean feral tomcat. He walked my brother and me to our one-room schoolhouse and escorted us back at end of the day.

Everything started to change. The little school was closed, and I got bussed to the nearby town of Utica, an hour and a half each way. There was more tension in the house; Dad was getting angry a lot. Suddenly we moved to Rochester into an old house that was converted into two apartments, one upstairs and one downstairs. It bordered on a semi-industrial part of southwest Rochester, but just two blocks away was the ritzy part of town where all the doctors from the Mayo Clinic lived. I was embarrassed about where we lived, and I hated my dad's awful pink-and-white Hudson. If he took me somewhere, I made him drop me off a block away. Where did this come from? I was so awkward. I got all dressed up in my best outfit and went to a girl classmate's birthday party. I rang the bell, she opened the door, and said, "The party was *last night"* and slammed the door. I stood there holding the present with my hair all combed in my light blue pressed pants and shirt. I was devastated. I felt really stupid.

My paper route included "Pill Hill," where all the doctors lived. Somebody would let their St. Bernard/Pit Bull mix out almost every morning. Appearing out of nowhere, that big red dog would come snarling for me. I would try to fend him off with a bat, but it seemed like at least once a week my pants would get torn or I got bitten. I was afraid to tell anyone, so I got grounded frequently for wrecking my clothes. I hated big dogs!

I think every kid has one of *those* summers. The family was taking a road trip to Pierre, South Dakota, to see my other grandparents, my dad's folks. We didn't get to see much of them, but this grandpa always smelled like leather and tobacco, and every time he saw me he gave me a silver dollar. Grandma was always dressed up and had a bologna roll hairdo. They loved to ride horses in fancy English outfits.

Sitting in the backseat of the Chrysler, my brother, Bobby, pulled out the cigarette lighter and put it on his tongue. Pushing it all the way back in, he said to me, "Boy that tastes funny. Why don't you try it?" I pulled it out and stuck it on my tongue. Instantly the car was filled with the stink of burnt flesh. I had a scar for years.

The day after we got there, we all went to a rodeo in Fort Pierre, about ten miles away. At one point in the festivities, I saw an old Indian riding up in a buckboard wagon pulled by a horse with his woman walking behind. It didn't seem right to me, so I jumped up to go and tell him what I thought. Dad got me by the scruff of the neck just before I got to the Indian and said I should probably leave them alone.

As we were heading back to Grandpa and Grandma's house, we stopped for ice cream. Bobby and I got in the back of the station wagon. Off we drove up the hill, and Bobby somehow unlatched the back door. I fell out and rolled all the way back down to the bottom. I was all scraped and lumpy, bleeding here and there, but I never let go of that ice cream cone. After they got me cleaned up and bandaged, my throat started to swell. I had gotten the mumps. What a summer adventure for me!

My South Dakota grandpa was a dentist, and they lived in a huge house. He was a very lucky man. He traded shares in a Yukon gold mine with a patient, and they struck gold two weeks later. Grandma sent him to the market one day for some essentials she forgot. He *never* went to the grocery store, but he was the 100,000th person through the door. He won a brand new Packard convertible full of groceries. He did the *New York Times* crossword puzzle in ink and won on a regular basis. This grandma was an artist. She made the most wonderful marionettes. My favorites were Mahatma Gandhi and Winston Churchill. What a generous, wonderful family.

Sometime after our move to Rochester, Grandpa Fifield died, and Dad had to rush out to South Dakota to get Grandma. She went kind of crazy and started taking everything in the house to the dump—silver tea sets, antique furniture, everything of value. Dad got her back to Rochester and moved her into a little house behind our place. One afternoon, all hell broke loose. There were police, ambulances, sirens, and people running all over the place. Nobody ever talked about what happened, but piecing it together later, she committed suicide. There was an empty bottle of booze and an empty bottle of pills, her wrists were slit, and her head was in the gas oven. She didn't die on the scene but later in the hospital. I felt so strange and empty. Why didn't anyone talk about this? I don't remember a service or anyone mentioning her again for years. One minute she was here and the next gone.

Soon we moved to a huge, amazing old farmhouse on three acres of land in northwest Rochester close to John Marshall High School. Mother had a big garden out back; Bob and I each had our own rooms upstairs, along with Dad's new painting studio. The house was so big that the back half of the upstairs was closed off and used to store Dad's paintings. The house was surrounded by a full acre of lawn. Dad, Bob, and I took turns mowing it. By the time we finished one end, it was time to start back at the other end. Every Saturday morning we would clean house while Mom baked for the week. Our special treat for cleaning was homemade sweet rolls. My God, my mouth is watering right now! All of Bob's and my friends would show up about 10:00 a.m. to help us take care of this abundance problem.

The place was beautiful. It was filled with all my dad's paintings and my mom's decorating genius. We had mobs of friends and dinner parties with Mom's cooking, leaving everyone stuffed and amazed at how incredibly good the food was. My friends and I would sneak into Dad's studio to look for naked ladies in his art books.

Then came that life-changing day in the seventh-grade locker room. I was naked for the first time in gym class with all the other guys. It was cold, and I was a skinny little white kid with shriveled-up genitals and not a hair on my body from the eyebrows down. Next to me stood a fellow who had been held back *two* grades. His was hanging on the ground, and he was covered with hair. He looked at me and laughed. The thought came, *I will never measure up. I am totally inadequate.*

I was a mama's boy. I did what I was asked. I helped around the house and in the garden. By the time I was sixteen, I was involved with sports and other school activities, so I don't know why I was in a pool hall, and I had my first drink of alcohol. Somebody handed me a fifth of gin in a pool hall, and I drank the whole thing. Sometime later I came out of a blackout with a bunch of guys beating the hell out of me and my thought was, *My God, I waited all my life to feel like this!*

Now, I don't know about the rest of you guys, but when I was sixteen, I was so horny I thought it was going to kill me. Maybe I was going to die of an impacted erection or something. It would explode and take out a whole neighborhood. It would make the newspapers, and everybody would know. Two weeks after the drink in the pool hall, I ended up with a twenty-six-year-old girlfriend, so don't tell me that gin doesn't work. She showed me what to do with those straps in a Volkswagen Beetle. Why would I do anything else?

I stopped going home. There were no more sports or other school activities I rode around on "borrowed" motorcycles and stayed out all night. Party, party, party! Drinking, pills, and marijuana. For some reason, people were getting annoyed with me. My parents, teachers, and counselors and a few scrapes with the police all seemed to be telling me to leave town. Colorado State University in Fort Collins accepted me as a student. I decided to go to Colorado.

Now I was standing in front of a Laundromat in Blunt, South Dakota, with my thumb out. Up pulled a '49 Hudson. I got in, and it was full of whiskey and Indians. Off we roared into the night. We drove all night long. The sun started coming up, and they pulled over to let me out. I fell from the car, too drunk to stand. Looking up, I saw the Laundromat they picked me up in front of the night before. It seems that this is an analogy for addiction: you ain't going anywhere—you're just going around the block. The trick is to recognize your stop. I missed my stop for the next thirty years.

CHAPTER THREE

Air Force Brat—Sandy

"My greatest fear is that I'm not enough, the truth is that I am not enough to control everything."

"If I choose wrong, I get to choose again."
—Sandy

As the child of a career military fighter pilot living near a U.S. Air Force base and going to school with other children of military personnel, I became aware of the impermanence of life very early. Other children in school would go away because their fathers didn't come home. Maybe they died in a plane crash, some other kind of accident, or war. Being a fighter pilot was a dangerous job, and we all knew it. Some of the other mothers just couldn't handle the uncertainty, but my mother could. I was proud of her, but in a way, I hated her independence, her ability to keep things together and to take care of me, my sister, and two brothers. I was the oldest and took responsibility for far too much.

From Clearwater Beach, Florida, where I was born, to El Paso, Texas, from Riverside, California, back to Reading, Massachusetts, on to Montgomery, Alabama, to Terre Haute, Indiana, and London, England. We moved every couple of years to my father's new assignment. This always meant new schools and new friends. Somewhere on this journey I became shy—painfully shy. The whole world and especially people scared me. I have come to realize that shy could be defined as self-centered and scared shitless. That was certainly true for me.

I thought that my father was the most romantic and wonderful being on earth; to fly jet airplanes was what I wanted to do as well. Then society made it very clear to me that girls could not even dream of becoming a jet pilot. This was in the 1950s when career choices for girls were limited, to say the least. I was resentful of the double standard, but it didn't cause me to work harder to achieve the impossible. I gave up but kept the resentment buried in my fear.

The "worst" summer of my young life happened in Reading, Massachusetts. While my father was gone to the Korean War, we lived in a small house on a hill. There was a huge woods out back and a farm across the street. A series of mishaps live in my memory. I chased a ball into a large patch of poison ivy and had to spend a week in a bath of Epsom salts. A bumblebee stung me on the end of my nose, leaving with me with a red ping-pong ball nose in the middle of my face. As I sang the ditty, "Fatty, fatty, two by four, couldn't get through the bathroom door" to the fat girl down the street, I sat on a large wasp. That cut my singing short for sure. Then the boy next door offered me a ride on his bike. As I sat on the handlebars, he boasted to me that we were not going to stop at the busy crossroads at the bottom of the hill. To prevent this, I stuck my foot into the spokes of the front wheel. We flipped end over end and crashed off the side of the road. My foot was mangled, and his bike was a total wreck. He was not happy with me, and his parents wouldn't buy him a new bike. I healed from these adventures with no lasting effects except maybe to learn that teasing could bring instant results.

I was always a seeker of the truth even though my parents were not particularly religious. My father was quite the skeptic, believing in science and rational thinking. He probably would have described himself as agnostic. They got married in a Unitarian church. As I grew up, we went to church on Easter and maybe even Christmas. We went to whatever church there was on base, sometimes Baptist, maybe Episcopalian, occasionally Presbyterian—basically Christian. My brother and I were allowed to do what we wanted. If it was available, we went to vacation Bible school. If we had friends who went to Sunday school, we could as well.

An enduring memory is a Sunday when I was eight years old in South Carolina. We lived in a small subdivision near Shaw Air Force Base. There was a tiny white-painted church in the middle of the field near our house. My brother and I decided to go to a Sunday service. Our mother dressed us up and sent us off with a smile. We went inside and sat down near the middle of the church, not knowing what to expect. From the pulpit a man started screaming and gesturing, accusing us of sin and degradation. He was a real Southern Baptist "hellfire and brimstone" preacher. We were horrified. We looked each other, got down on the floor, crawled out of the church, and ran crying all the way home. This was my last church experience for quite a while.

We sometimes got to spend long summers on Cape Cod with relatives. During the summer of 1956, my cousins had a house in Plymouth, Massachusetts, right at the start of the long spit of sand across Plymouth Bay. It was a huge, old historic house, and they arranged for us to have one also. There was a beach club with a swimming pool and tennis courts, and the ocean beach was just over the sand dunes. Our fathers were away working but would spend as much time as possible with us. They read us stories of pirates and treasure and embellished these with their own tales of buried treasure in their youth.

One morning my father took my brother and me upstairs into a dark old closet and shined a light on a discovery—a skull and crossbones burned into the wood and an arrow pointing upward. Pirates! Treasure! We followed the arrows into the attic, where we found a really old-looking map on a piece of paper stuffed into a corked bottle hidden away in the rafters. We were ecstatic! A treasure map! We rushed outside to find our cousins, who were rushing to find us. Their father had shown them a similar clue at their house. The maps had to be used together to find the treasure hidden somewhere in the vicinity. After running us all around the neighborhood following clues for about four hours, we ended up on the beach. We finally marked off the exact spot where the treasure was buried and started to dig into the sand. We were five kids caught in the throes of excitement and greed. The "treasure" was down about three feet in the sand. We nearly gave up when one of us stuck the top of a chest. It was about one foot by two feet and looked like a real treasure chest. We fell on it, screaming and kicking each other, and pulled it out of the hole. Later on the living room floor we negotiated the division of the spoils. There were toys, jewels, candy gold pieces, and real money. The summer was an idyll for all of us filled with new discoveries and puberty just around the corner.

Next we moved to Terre Haute, Indiana, a small city with no air force base nearby. My father was assigned to an U.S. Air National Guard unit for three years. Beginning with sixth grade, I finished junior high. Two new beings appeared in my consciousness: horses and boys. Because we were settled for three whole years, my parents bought me a horse. We became urban ranchers. My horse gave me freedom—freedom to be out by myself, freedom to start seeing boys secretly, freedom to learn to swear like a sailor, and freedom to acquire a "reputation."

I went through all the normal agonies of early puberty. I demanded to know when I could start shaving my legs, using makeup, and wearing tight clothes so I could be more attractive to boys. It's a lucky thing we left Indiana before I started high school. It would have been a disaster given the start I had made for myself. Our three years were up, and now we were on our way to England for four years. High school here I come!

I attended Bushy Park American High School, London, England, in the late fall of 1958. We Americans didn't attend English schools because they didn't prepare us for college back in the States. As I started my freshman year, I was back with the jaded kids of military personnel. My shyness really became intense; I seemed to be afraid of everything. I wanted so badly to have friends and be social. I found the kids who were not popular but who accepted my fear and me.

We discovered quite early and easily that the Brits had virtually no age limit laws concerning alcohol at all. Everything was available, but we soon moved from hard cider and beer to hard liquor because it works so much faster. London and its suburbs became our playground. Since none of us had a car and we didn't live near each other, we rode the subway and buses to each other's houses to have all-night parties. Hopefully no parents would be there.

At one of these parties, I have a vivid memory of kneeling in front of the liquor cabinet, discovering a bottle of vodka, upending it, and guzzling the whole thing. It felt like a miracle. It took away my shyness and all memory for a while. It took me away. I loved it. On the bus to school the next day, I heard whispering all around me.

They were saying, "Sandy is a lush." I had only a vague idea of what that meant, but I knew I didn't want that term applied to me. I got sneaky. I had to have a guy who liked to drink so I could drink and not be blamed. I stole scotch from my father's liquor cabinet and brought it to school in my perfume bottle with a little perfume mixed in so it didn't smell like scotch. I drank every chance I got. I loved the parties and the effects of alcohol. I was set free from me. My other addiction was love, and I loved the bad boys.

After high school and back in the States, I went to college at Eastern New Mexico University. I immediately found the new students who were *not* from Portales, Clovis, or anywhere in New Mexico or Texas who all seemed hopelessly rural and cowboy. Not for me. I was worldly and sophisticated. I fell in love once, twice, three times. I fell in love again, this time with David from New York City. Needless to say, I knew nothing about sex and birth control. I just kind of hoped that nothing would happen. "They" said it usually didn't happen the first time you did "it." I'd always been careful about "going all the way," but now I took a chance—he was the one. After the school year, we traveled to New York in his Plymouth Fury station wagon. My intent was to become a career girl in the big city. Then I found out I was pregnant. Surprise!

We flew to Denver to meet with my mother, and she was not happy. I thought at the time she was angry with me, but I later found out she was angry at the injustice of it all. Marriage to David was out of the question for me. New York seem like a foreign country, and I had discovered that David was really very selfish and a mama's boy. He didn't want to marry me either, which suited us both just fine.

I stayed with my family who had moved to Denver. We didn't find it necessary for me to go away to an unwed mother's home. Since we were new to the community, we could concoct any story we wanted. Mine was that my husband had been killed in Vietnam, and now here I was, left alone and pregnant to start over. That was exactly what I planned to do. I resigned myself to the fact that I was going to have a baby. This was meant to be, and it was time to accept this reality. My parents accepted this with grace and good humor. We did have fun with it. I enjoyed my pregnancy, but deep inside I knew that I could not raise this child on my own. I decided I would give my baby up for adoption. I made this decision because I knew that I was still too selfish and self-centered. Heck, I wanted to party some more. I had been removed from the fun for nearly a year, and I wanted to get back into life, but I truly wanted to give my baby the best chance I could.

I gave birth February 5, 1965, to a beautiful baby boy who I saw and held once, but my mind was made up, and I have never regretted this decision.

CHAPTER FOUR

Our Life Together

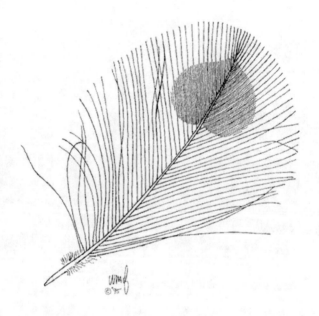

"The reason for a relationship is not to make us happy; it is meant to show us who we are."
—Bill

I was starting school again at Colorado State University (CSU) in Fort Collins. My mother had finally gone, and I walked across the campus. There he was—a god walking toward me, tall and handsome, wearing little Abner boots (World War I combat boots). It electrified me. How was I ever going to meet this guy?

No problem, there he was at the freshman mixer! Wow, he was going to school here also. I was in heaven. He saw me across the room, came over to me, and commanded, "Choose me!" And I did! It was even better that he said he was an artist and wanted to draw me nude. I said, "Okay," and off we went to his motel. So much for good intentions, of finally making something of myself. I was off again. I was in love!

He said his name was William Theodore Harrison Fifield III but I could call him Bill.

Now our story becomes one.
We are started on our great adventure!

We started classes and partying with great enthusiasm. Bill started art classes but soon clashed with the instructor and left school within the first month. He stayed around, though, and got a room and a job at the off-campus T-shirt shop. Sandy lived in the dorm. We decorated Bill's room with a wall-sized collage of magazine pictures and acquired a blue-eyed Siberian husky puppy.

Sandy was fascinated by the artist but kept complaining she couldn't draw this, couldn't do that, couldn't, couldn't, couldn't, and on and on ad nausea! This pissed Bill off, so he handed Sandy a beer coaster with a Coors lion on it and said, "I don't want to see you again until you draw this!" Sandy took it to her dorm room and worked on it like a demon. She returned with an 8" x 11" drawing. Bill was very impressed. Our partnership as artists had begun.

So how do we write an observational narrative by us and about us? What was Sandy's dependence? She hung on Bill's every word, mood, likes, and dislikes, sleeping in the same bed, barely able to move for fear of waking him. She would gaze at him while he was driving, thinking, *If there ever comes a day when he says he doesn't love me, I will not be able to go on living.* She felt like a Victorian heroine who could take to her bed and die of a broken heart.

Despite Sandy's overdependence on Bill, we started with a very different vision of what our relationship could be. We would be partners and would share everything: responsibilities, money, and creative ideas. We would be artists together. Where is the model for this kind of journey? We had no guide, but we went anyway, and we have never let up. We have never stopped forging this path. We have dug deep in one place, starting with our relationship. There have been obstacles and alluring bypaths on this pilgrimage.

It wasn't too long till Sandy missed her period. It seemed a mystery to us. "They" said that pregnancy usually didn't happen within the first year of giving birth. We thought we were safe! Obviously we didn't know anything about birth control. Sandy went to a local doctor to check it out. He was Catholic and was rather horrified at our request for a solution. He was certain that we should get married and raise a family, but we had other ideas. It wasn't until Bill got threatening that he came up with the name of an illegal abortionist in Denver, along with the promise of a cleanup operation if anything went wrong. Neither of us was particularly upset with this—scared, yes, but we did know that we were not ready to have a family. After it was over, we went back to this doctor for "The Pill." He tried refusing again, to no avail, and we got a prescription for birth control pills. Now for the first time we could have sex with no consequences. We felt great freedom. We had a modern relationship. Now Sandy had control of her own destiny and body. Those early birth control pills had enough hormones in them to keep an elephant from getting pregnant.

Then there was Fort Collins' first dope ring to participate in. This set the tone that we could act any way or do anything we wanted with no consequences—smoking marijuana, underage drinking, and sex. Everyone in the house we were living in got arrested but us; we were in Aspen selling some marijuana. Sandy finished out the school year, but there was no more college for us.

Off we went to Denver, abandoning the wreckage behind us, where we each got straight jobs in downtown, Bill to work in the linen department of a large store and Sandy in a magazine sales office where she got to browbeat people into buying magazine subscriptions. We made enough money to buy a 1958 blue green Opel sedan for about $300. It looked like a daisy duck car. We now had another new freedom; we could hang around Sixteenth Street after work where the cruising scene was in 1966. We discovered a wonderful store featuring custom-made jewelry. We had to meet the artist! We hit it off, and he offered to teach us how to cast our own creations. He also introduced us to all kinds of artistic people in Denver. He knew the actors and artists involved at Denver's only avante garde theater, the Trident. We were invited to the late-night post-show parties. With all kinds of new drugs to try, it got harder and harder to get up to go to those straight jobs.

Not surprisingly, we used Sandy's incredible innocent beauty to help open the doors to Denver's art scene. It worked! It seems every man has a plan, and we knew it! Our circle of friends exploded.

A college friend lived in Georgetown, Colorado. He said we could get jobs there. We decided, "Let's move to Georgetown!" We packed our few belongings and drove up in the Opel, our very cold home for two nights. Then we spent a night at the deputy sheriff's house, and we landed jobs at the Silver Queen Restaurant as bartender and waitress with a room to live in above the bar furnished with the noisiest antique bed ever made. This employment lasted about two months.

From the Silver Queen we moved to a tiny A-frame cabin outside of Georgetown, where we soon ran into trouble with the rent and moved into the Georgetown Motor Inn, where we worked as virtual slaves for a room to live in, food, and LSD. The owner had great connections for powerful psychedelic drugs that we helped to distribute and consume. By selling our jewelry creations at the bar of the Red Lion Restaurant, we were beginning to do quite well, we thought—well enough to buy pitchers of gin and tonic at the bar and act like big shots in town.

It became necessary to move back to Denver. We had exhausted our welcome and possibilities in Georgetown. We moved into a third-floor apartment in an old house on Capitol Hill behind the Aladdin Theater. Then we found a cute little bungalow on Williams Street, where we occupied the second-floor apartment for $45 a month. We were invited to try out for a play at the Trident. They needed a guard and a nun for the play, "The Persecution and Assassination of Marat/Sade," a dark social commentary that really seemed to fit the times. We earned a grand total of $30 a week between us.

My God, we really seemed to have arrived. We were smoking reefer, taking LSD, and feeling our whole bodies reverberate with the music and sex. We sure didn't seem to eat much; we must have been living on love. We never wanted it to end. We bought art books and supplies. We discovered Art Nouveau. Starting with cut-out tissue paper flowers, we were always creating something. We built a model of the studio/residence we would like to have one day. An octagon shape, it would contain all the tools and materials for anything an artist could dream of creating. It was truly and literally a "pipe-dream" for us then, but it almost perfectly came true in less than ten years.

After the three-month run of the play and coincidentally the end of the Trident Theater, we found our first studio. It was at Eleventh and Detroit Streets across from an old Denver fire station. It was an old grocery store, and there was a big open room downstairs and apartment upstairs. We had collected a few old tools, and Bill even got a commission for an Art Nouveau table. It wasn't enough to sustain us, however. Salvation came in the form of a building contractor from the mountains who wanted us to help complete a custom home he was building in Dillon, Colorado. Bill was to create custom kitchen cabinets, as well as a hand-carved front door. Sandy painted a life-sized mural of huge, bright flowers on the dining room wall. We agreed to do this for room and board and a little money. But this couldn't last.

We had a disagreement with the contractor, and off we went, back to Denver.

Here we went again. It seemed we were continually being taken advantage of. First we put ourselves in a compromising position, and then we got resentful when we were used and discarded. We kept waiting for people to see what geniuses we were and reward us. Never once did we make sure the terms were clear. Our business skills were woefully inadequate. We felt that we should have been plucked from obscurity and transformed into world-famous artists with no effort on our part beyond making beautiful things.

We were living in a dream world of drugs and alcohol. We had no idea what addiction really was either. There were so many new drugs to try as well as booze to drink. We agreed that we would never mess with those addictive drugs such as heroin; we were way too protective of ourselves, and we felt we were too smart to get addicted to anything. Booze, pot, speed, psychedelics, and cigarettes—we could control those. They would never rule us! Besides, if we got addicted we would just quit, since we were told and believed that these drugs were only psychologically addicting.

Alcohol and drugs took the place of God; they became the solution. They were truly a higher power. We surrounded ourselves with hedonists and intellectuals who fueled the belief that drugs and alcohol were to path to enlightenment. We dabbled in atheism and existentialism without ever really understanding these philosophies. We absolutely believed Timothy Leary when he said it was possible to use drugs to reach the other side and stay there, now a perfect human being. Today we realize this is probably not what he meant, but then we bought it hook, line, and sinker. We wanted the easy way to Nirvana.

Sandy found herself caught up in bewilderment and despair—everything seemed absurd. What was the use of living or even breathing? Then a strange thing happened. Like magic, a TV arrived in our studio, a black cube on which an angel appeared: J. Krishnamurti, an Indian spiritual teacher. He brought a message of hope and spirituality. Then the TV was gone, but the feeling of hope remained to lift the veil of depression. However, this did not mean the end of drug and alcohol use for us, nor did we become devotees of this spiritual teacher.

After a couple of more moves to work on other people's houses, we settled in an apartment at Third and Washington Streets. Sandy landed a lucrative waitressing job at the Bratskeller in Larimer Square. Bill hooked up with a couple of fellows who had a studio on Curtis Street in Auraria near downtown Denver and needed a woodworker to complement their metal work. With all the new ideas, tools, and materials to be explored, Bill threw himself into this exciting new phase. There were lots of jobs and working with other artists, but once again nothing was really made clear, and Sandy felt left out of the studio equation.

The job at the Bratskeller brought in great money but not a lot of artistic satisfaction. This wasn't in our vision of how things might be in our relationship, so Sandy decided to go to art/jewelry school in San Miguel de Allende, Mexico, to further her skills in jewelry making and to gain the confidence to join the crew at the studio on Curtis Street.

Lucky thing we had an open relationship—as soon as Sandy left for Mexico, Bill found a girlfriend, but he wasn't the only one. Sandy found a boyfriend within two days. They were flings for each of us, but we both knew that's all it was. We were looking forward to being together again. Oddly enough, very little jealousy occurred. We found out how much we loved each other.

A more lasting consequence came from the fact that Sandy mailed an ounce of marijuana from Mexico. Thinking what? This is a good idea? Sandy's brother really paid the price for this clever move, since he was in our apartment when the package arrived. Surprise! He got six months in Denver County Jail, but we just got a year's probation with one night in jail. Once again we skated on the edge of disaster, never really taking responsibility for our actions.

Because of the lack clarity in the business situation at the studio, the partnership of artists terminated in a big argument, leaving us with the building on Curtis Street to ourselves. We immediately moved into the upstairs apartment and renamed it "The Studio." The commissions started to pour in. We worked all day and night, drinking all day, using speed all night to get some work done. By this time we had acquired our own woodworking and jewelry-making tools. We were set to take off.

Dig Deep in One Place

Once again we had arrived; artists from all over Denver made The Studio a regular stop. We produced all kinds of beautiful stuff; creativity abounded from the place. We had a cooler of gin and tonic going at all times, and drugs were easy to come by. The party was constant.

Why were we so selfish and self-centered? The answer was simple: because it seemed to work. All evidence seemed to point to the fact that we came out on top.

But this couldn't last either; we only had the place for two years when Denver Urban Renewal (DURA) offered us a good sum of money to leave. Our neighborhood was to be turned into the Auraria Campus of the University of Colorado. Actually, they came to our rescue because The Studio scene was getting too expensive; mentally, physically and emotionally. Using the cash DURA gave us as a down payment and with a lot of help from Sandy's mother to qualify for a mortgage, we decided to buy our own place.

After looking around Denver at some truly awful properties, we decided to look in the foothills southwest of Denver where some friends had already purchased property. In Conifer we found a ten—acre ranch with a 50' x 50' metal horse barn and two small houses. Perfect; we could convert the barn for use as a studio. It was a mess, but we had great fun cleaning and tearing out the horse stalls, using the lumber for benches, insulating the place, and installing two wood-burning stoves to make it a warm and cozy place to work even in winter. We worked hard on the houses, using one to live in and one to rent.

Here was our fantasy home and studio. We had gathered all kinds of great tools for our jewelry, metalwork, woodworking, and glasswork, just like our dream had foretold.

Now everything could get back to normal (whatever that was). We would be able to concentrate on our work. First we decided to have a party and invite all our friends from Denver! So the party continued.

Sandy's work turned from jewelry to stained glass, and we began to combine glass, woodworking and metal together. Huge oak doors filled with beveled glass, stained glass windows, hand-carved trim around everything, exotic furniture, and cabinets—there seemed to be no end to the ideas and projects. We made a good living from our work. We became successful artists.

Despite the fact we were making more money, we still had difficulty taking real responsibility by paying the mortgage with consistency. There seemed to be many more important things to buy, such as booze, shoes, food, and of course, drugs. By this time, methedrine (speed) had become almost impossible for us to get, but a new drug appeared on the scene—cocaine. It seemed to be the perfect solution. Along with alcohol, you could work and party for days on end, and our friends/employers seem to have an endless supply. We thought we were cheating time.

It seemed all our friends were getting married. We decided to as well. We wanted to have another big party and receive gifts too. We actually tried to start a family, but the Universe had other ideas. Years of heavy-duty birth control and an illegal abortion had taken their toll. This is probably the only thing we paid the consequences for: the inability to have a family.

Oh well, on to bigger and better art. We worked for a rich client in a Colorado ski resort with plenty of money and cocaine to throw around, and we were ready to receive. Truthfully, some wonderful pieces of artwork were produced amongst the madness, like exotic carved doors, beveled window panels, and stained glass. One good thing that came from this was better tools and machinery to create these masterpieces.

This continued for a number of years, eventually degenerating into weeklong binges. We tacked up blackout curtains over our picture windows, and our parties became more solitary affairs with only one or two friends; we didn't want the night to end. Everything, jobs and pleasure, now seemed to be attached to the availability of cocaine. Of course alcohol was always there, a basic legal right of every adult American.

Then a real consequence of addiction showed up. After a long day of work, booze, and cocaine, Bill experienced an aneurysm (stroke) as he was sitting on the toilet. Pain like nothing he had ever experienced rose up his spine to explode in the back of his head. There was no paralysis, and he didn't die, so after a long discussion, we came to the conclusion that cocaine could kill you. So we decided to quit with the cocaine. The alcohol remained as a good consolation prize.

Recovery from this was going to take time, maybe a lot of time, so Sandy got a job at Safeway while friends visited Bill to console him with the alcohol he had demanded that they bring. It was a problem that was becoming obvious to everyone but us, so they eventually quit coming around.

By this time, Sandy's dependency had taken a drastic turn. Now she had to take control of everything—finances, food, driving, and how much liquor to bring home. Sandy never knew what she would be coming home to. It was getting increasingly difficult to control Bill's drinking and to find enough time for her own drinking.

We bought an old Scout for Bill to drive in an attempt to provide him with some freedom of movement for his work, but it ended up mostly being used to go to the liquor store while Sandy was at work. The focus of our lives became the drinking. Everything else fell away, even the sex because of the blood pressure medicine. Bill began making phone calls in his blackouts to old friends, including one in recovery who had the courage to call Sandy's mother and say that something had to be done or Bill would probably die from the physical effects of addiction, commit suicide, or hurt someone in his obsession.

Sandy's relief at having the truth revealed at last was as though she had been holding her breath for ten years and could finally exhale. She didn't know what would happen, but the solution was in sight. It started in the form of an intervention to confront Bill with his problems and asked if he would go into a treatment program at Harmony Foundation in Estes Park, Colorado.

PART TWO

What Happened

This is where our stories split into our separate paths to recovery using the Twelve Steps and a spiritual life while we continued our journey together.

CHAPTER FIVE

Arrival at the Temple, Bill—July 28, 1992, 6:05 p.m.

"How can you get anywhere if you
don't know where you are?"
—Bill

I entered the treatment center through the back door into the coffee room. The check-in by Vampire Bill, so called because all he did was take blood and blood pressure, was a little spooky. He literally had Coke-bottle glasses, and his nose about an inch from my arm. He suddenly stuck in a needle dead center into my vein.

"We will have to examine your belongings, please," said a sweet little nurse.

"You're looking at them," I said, standing there in a pair of too-small shorts, a really ugly Hawaiian shirt, and some smelly canvas deck shoes.

"Oh my, we don't allow shorts here." Thank God they cut me a little slack until I could get an essentials delivery. Without the shorts, the outfit would have been really bad. "Here, take this."

"What is it?"

"It will help you come down." I think it was Librium. When you drink a quart of vodka a day before noon for ten years, stopping abruptly might be a problem.

Heading for my room, I passed through the main lobby for the first time. Yikes! It was full of mounted animals. There was a full-size African elephant head mounted on the wall, a leopard crouched on the mantle staring at the phone, and a really angry baboon in the rafters. Boy, was I glad I was not coming out of a blackout sitting in that lobby.

"Put your stuff in the room and head for the dining room." I did what I was told. The days were very structured. I wasn't very hungry, but that would change, as the food was excellent. I had to stay in the main lodge for about a week so they could keep an eye on me. I wasn't allowed out, there were no phone calls for the first week, and you could only smoke in the coffee room or outside. Did I say I had never before done what I'd been told? I did as well as I could to follow the rules. My roommate hated me. He said I snored—really snored. I didn't believe him. I never heard it, but the circumstantial evidence was adding up. Early every morning the yard was full of bull elk. My enthusiastic snores sucked them right out of the woods, as if I was a threat to their harems.

My counselor was four foot eight. She was a gin-drinking, Camel-smoking firecracker, about sixty years old—my kind of woman. She stood in front of me—I'm six foot four—shaking her finger under my nose, saying, "We don't need another damn genius in recovery; we need someone to wash the cups." After a bit of a protest about my sensitive artist hands, I washed my first load of cups. Something remarkable happened. At that moment, the obsession was lifted. For the first time since I was a kid, I had done something for someone else with no strings attached. I wash cups to this day.

After seven days, I was let out for a walk. Around the outside of the compound, about one mile, I went with ten or twelve other clients. They were all slightly ahead of me when I spotted a ratty old magpie feather on the ground. I bent down and picked it up. At that moment, all the other folks turn in unison as if choreographed by the Rockettes. To a person, they all thought that feather appeared magically in my hand. "How did you do that?" they said with huge eyes. I looked at them with huge eyes and was overwhelmed with the realization: "My God, I'm obsessed. I'm an addict. I'm afraid. I'm dangerous! If I don't change what I'm doing right now, somebody is going to die. Not me, somebody else." I would come out of a blackout with somebody stuck to the fender of my Scout. It was so clear it hurt. Fifteen minutes later in a group therapy session, I opened my mouth and out poured the horror of my life. I spoke for an hour and fifteen minutes; I couldn't stop. I started to cry. It seemed like for the next six months I couldn't open my mouth without crying. I wasn't allowed to watch Puppy Chow commercials. "The puppies are so cute! Sob, sob!" I didn't realize it at the time, but I just did the first five steps of the Twelve Step program. My counselor noticed immediately and changed to being my sponsor on the spot. "Something miraculous has happened to you, and I hope to God you can keep it!" she said.

We turned our focus from the treatment center stuff to understanding the Steps. "This isn't about you anymore," she said, holding up the *Big Book,* alcoholics' fond name for the book of Alcoholics Anonymous. "The whole first part of this book is about helping someone else. From the front cover to the top of page twenty-three it tells us over twenty-three times you have to help someone else for permanent recovery. It doesn't mention alcohol specifically after page forty-three; instead it focuses on the delusion that we can somehow control our circumstances to protect ourselves from our fear. It becomes an obsession to make our individual worlds safe and predictable. Whatever the substance or behavior, the result is that our world narrows to just that. The *Big Book* tells us that we can recover from this seemingly hopeless state of mind and body. As a matter of fact, it says recovered sixteen times and recovering only once. The book also says we can never safely indulge in our obsessions in any form at all, ever."

I remember my first call to Sandy. "I'm going to do this, damn it! I can't believe there's a way out." The days were filled with lots of writing and group sessions. It was so wonderful to be away from the madness, to be able to concentrate on turning in a different direction. There were about fifty people going through the treatment center at the same time as me. Some of them were even sicker than me! Almost every human on this earth is afflicted with the spiritual disease of fear to some extent or another unless we have learned a different way. About one person in ten actually develops an addiction or obsession.

These Twelve Steps aren't for people who need them or for people who want them; they are for folks who do them. At first introduction, all this looked like Chinese to me. I mean it. I could read the words, but nothing registered. It took me years of taking protégés through the Steps before they really made sense and got really simple. At first all I could do was follow directions, and because of that, something started to happen. I started to change. It was working in spite of me.

The first time Sandy saw me after dropping me off at Harmony, she was shocked. This was ten days later. Although I was eating like a horse, I had dropped a ton of weight, and my stride and demeanor must have changed a lot. I was still scared but thrilled that I had a solution. I would be scared for a while, but now I had purpose and meaning and direction.

Sandy came back for family week, and I think she wished she hadn't. I've never seen her so mad. We had decided quite some time before that I was the problem, so when they told her she might have a problem as well, she got furious. Talk about confusing. I never noticed her behavior much. She was always the designated driver. Besides—in the group therapy session with the family, they all got to say what they thought of us and we got to make an amends of sorts. I learned as much from the other families as they did from Sandy. Never had I been told what I looked like before. I did not know how scary I was. At the end I must have looked like some spawn of Satan. There were no whites of my eyes; because of all the broken blood vessels, they were fire engine red. People would look me in the eye and quickly step back.

The time to leave Harmony was coming, and stories were circulating about all the graduates who were relapsing. What would I do without the safety and discipline of this place? What if I suddenly had a drink in my hand? I could see that my counselor was worried also. "You must go to a meeting and get a sponsor immediately! You're only on Step Six, and you must continue." I wanted to stay so bad; they kicked me out a day early. It was Thursday after lunch and time to go. "Home." I just wanted to go home. But Thursday was Aftercare day in Boulder. The Aftercare program provided by Harmony went on every Thursday for three months, so going home and missing the first one would be okay, wouldn't it? *No!* This seemingly insignificant decision to go to Boulder and hang out until Aftercare set the tone for my whole recovery. Don't do what you want; do what you need to do. Placing my recovery first has paid bigger dividends than any other thing on my spiritual journey. Thank you, Universe, for the willingness.

Every day for the next six months I found a feather on the ground wherever I was. I believe the Higher Power was reminding me to recall the day at Harmony when the feather triggered a spiritual awakening in me. Sandy found them as well. At the end of our first year in recovery, we had enough feathers to build our own bird.

Going to the Twelve Step fellowship club near my house wouldn't be my first meeting. That had been at the treatment center on Tuesday nights. Groups nearby would bring a meeting in and run it. The club was right across Highway 285 from where we live, so we could walk. It seems I wasn't about to get sober till it was convenient. Carrying my *Big Book,* we set out and walked by a bunch of cowboys beating up on some cows next door. "Going to do a little light reading?" one of them asked.

"Yeah," I answered. "Care to join us?"

Never mind, I'm on a mission. Stepping through the clubhouse door, I saw a fellow I know. He said, "What the hell are you doing here?" Nice greeting.

"How about I'm never leaving." He's long gone, and we're still there. From that moment, the greeting from me has been, "Welcome, I'm so glad you're here."

A sponsor is theoretically someone who has been through the Steps and who can guide someone else through them. I asked for a sponsor at that first meeting and a guy comes up and says, "I'll be your sponsor."

Oh boy! Now we can really get somewhere! "What you want me to do?" I asked.

"Well, read the *Big Book* and go to meetings." I thought there was more to it. "There, there you'll be fine." So I averaged about nine meetings a week. Actually, I averaged nine meetings a week for the first ten years and listened to a lot of people share about recovery. It turns out I was right; there is a lot more to it. After about a month, this first sponsor took a job in Antarctica! I didn't think I was that bad, though I did pester him about recovery a lot.

My second sponsor was just as bad. "Just don't indulge and go to meetings." The one difference was he had me call him every day. That was a big improvement, but I still made no movement on the Steps. Three months later, he moved to Florida. I must have been getting better, because that wasn't nearly as far as the bottom of the earth. Watching and listening, it was clear nobody except one person had a clue what they were talking about. Some guys were bragging that they had never done the Steps. There sat a woman with ten years of recovery, meeting after meeting talking about her higher power, talking about happy, joyous freedom, and talking about doing the Steps. But she wouldn't sponsor men even though her first sponsor was a man. I started to call her. Taking a clue from sponsor number two, I started to call her every day and ask questions. Her ten years of experience shone through like a gem in this mess of personal opinions and bullshit. She shared her experience, and it brought strength and hope to me.

CHAPTER SIX

Resistance—Sandy

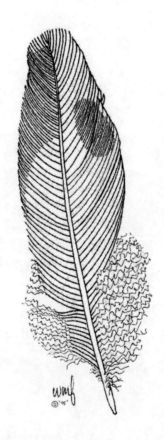

"Who would I be if I didn't believe the lie?"
—Sandy

Bill called after seven days at Harmony and said, "I'm going to do this thing, damn it!" I didn't know what to think. I just knew that my universe had changed—forever. The following Saturday, I drove up to visit. I saw Bill walk across the lawn towards me, an old familiar lightness in his step. My heart leapt! He looked different—slimmer yes, but healthier as well. Before his skin had looked so tight it was going to pop. The bloated look was gone. Here was a person I hadn't seen in years. We had a long talk sitting out at a picnic table in front of the building. He acknowledged the fact that indeed he had a problem and reaffirmed that he was going to do everything that was asked of him at Harmony. We came again to the conclusion that I had no problem with drugs or alcohol. I drove home after Saturday night dinner with the feeling that all was really right with the world, with a renewed sense of hope and optimism.

The next Sunday I was on my way to Harmony again, this time for family week. It was five days of treatment for family members meant to initiate them into this new lifestyle and partly to educate us on our own parts in this very human dance of addiction and recovery. My roommate was a woman who was the girlfriend of one of the clients; she just couldn't or wouldn't admit to any part in the problem. The group of people I was there with was very diverse. There were all sorts of new terms and ideas for us to learn and get used to. One of the most baffling of the new ideas was gratitude. What did I have to be grateful for? We were asked to write a gratitude list of twelve items we could be thankful for. I thought, *Well, I guess I can be grateful that I'm not on fire, that the list is only twelve items long, that I am alive, for my dogs, my parents, my life, and of course I am grateful for my womanly thighs, and five more.* Then we were told that we would read this in front of the group. I protested but was persuaded to do it anyway, to the great amusement of everyone.

The leader of our group began to focus on me. She thought I should take a certain test to determine my susceptibility to obsession and addiction. Feeling I was certainly not an addict of any kind, I agreed. The test showed a high susceptibility to addiction, and she suggested that I might have a problem myself. I was outraged. I had read books on addiction/obsession, and it wasn't me! We, Bill and I, had decided I was okay! What the hell was this? Talk about denial; I just couldn't shut up. "Well," the counselor said, "prove you do not have a problem. Why don't you stop drinking for three months as a start?"

I said, "No problem. I'll show you. That's right—give me a dare! I've got enough willpower to do this."

"Very well," she said. "Now how many fellowship meetings will you go to a week?" I thought three per week were just too many and asking way too much. Two seemed wimpy, so I said, "I promise I will go to one a week for three months."

"That will do," she said.

I was beginning to feel as though I had leapt up into a huge locomotive and started it up when I had staged the intervention; now here I was sitting on the tracks about to have it run over me. My world was changing with astonishing speed.

My roommate didn't fall for this trick, but today I'm glad I did, because when I got home from family week, I remembered my promise and after much fear and resistance, got myself to a meeting at a church about five miles from home that I was sure I would not be able to find. I didn't want to go to the Twelve Step fellowship club that was right across the highway from my house. I couldn't go there; I might see someone I knew. At this first meeting were approximately eight much older-looking men who told their stories. I left there with my brain on fire. I had identified with each of them—not the details but the feelings and reactions each of them had. I came home, and all the anger that had been building in me spilled over as I stood out back of my house and just screamed at the universe, at the unfairness of life, how everyone had

Dig Deep in One Place

failed me and how God himself had failed me. It was just luck that we had no close neighbors and the cops weren't called. Finally I just wound down exhausted but somehow very hopeful. My denial had started to be uncovered, and I was beginning to see I had always hid my alcohol and drug use behind someone who was worse than I was, who was bigger and louder about it, and whose behavior I could focus on trying to control. It had worked for so many years. Now I had to give this up? Now what the hell was I going to do? Well, I had promised I would go to one meeting a week, and I keep my promises.

Bill was to come home in a week, so I went for one more visit. On Thursday he could come home. I was excited and scared. Where would we have lunch? There was nothing but bars in Estes Park, or so it seemed, but we need lunch, so we stopped in a bar, both of us scared to death. We somehow lived through it without ordering a beer. Whew, first test over. Then we went on to Boulder. It was Aftercare night, so we stayed in Boulder to attend. Aftercare is a service provided by Harmony Foundation as part of treatment after the twenty-eight-day inpatient program ends. It takes place once a week for eight weeks. We hung out for four hours watching the drunks in Boulder's City Park. Finally Aftercare was over and we could go home. It was hard to make this choice but extremely important. It set the pattern for our recovery. We had to do it even if we didn't really feel like it.

Now it was Friday night. There was a meeting at the fellowship club across the highway at eight o'clock. I had always wondered what the place was. Was it a mountain-climbing club? If so, why were there cars in the parking lot every night? Now I knew. We walked over, with Bill carrying his *Big Book* with the cover turned outward, title blaring our purpose. We walked past the cowboys next door who were having a little informal rodeo and drinking beer. Talk about embarrassing. I asked if he could turn the book around, and he said, "No, I could not." One of the cowboys made some smart remark about light reading. Bill said, "I'm going to a meeting. Want to come along?"

We arrived at the fellowship club, soon to be our spiritual home. Yes, there were some folks I knew from the community. There was an acquaintance who had disappeared from the party scene. I remember partying in her neighborhood with vast amounts of everything from cocaine to vodka. There was way too much of everything. I had wondered where she had gone. There she was a different person, a caring and compassionate person. I was amazed. I was welcomed warmly and encouraged to keep coming back. It didn't matter to them that I said I was just supporting my husband, who was an immediate and enthusiastic part of the group. I still wasn't sure. I wasn't sure if I belonged, wasn't sure if I had a problem, and wasn't sure if I trusted these folks. They all seemed too friendly and eager to help. How could they be so happy about this stuff? They said that they took borderline cases, that people who don't have a problem don't worry about it the way I did, and that it didn't matter anyway. Just keep coming back. When I was encouraged to speak, I would say things like, "I'm Sandy, and my husband's the problem" or "I'm Sandy, and maybe I have half a problem," much to their delight. They were taking away my points of resistance. I found myself going to many more than one meeting per week.

My "real problem" was that I was identifying with their stories of how they had felt and what they had done. I thought, *Oh I've felt like that, done that, and reacted like that.* What a dilemma! I tried everything to get someone at the club to tell me I had a problem or not. No one took the bait. The last drink I had was on August 6. That meant that on November 7 my three months would be up and I would have proved myself to not have a problem. I began to suspect that since it had been so easy to quit, maybe I didn't have a problem after all. It should be very difficult, shouldn't it? Around the end of month two, Bill and I were talking about the future, and I said I was looking ahead to the end of the three months when I could have a drink. Bill looked at me and stated very calmly, "If you want to continue to indulge in that obsession, I will not be here. My sobriety is the most important thing in my life." That stopped me right in my tracks; of course he wouldn't want me to continue to indulge.

At the end of the three months, I had a great thought. *I could have a drink or I could have the world. What is my choice to be?* My choice was that I wanted what I had seen and felt in the meetings more than anything, more than I wanted to drink, more than I wanted that drug, more than I wanted anything else ever. I had begun to feel at peace, freedom from

Dig Deep in One Place

fear, and a sense of belonging that I had never felt before. I knew I was still a long way from happy, joyous freedom, but I had to start. I decided that I would remain abstinent one more year. That night I said for the first time at a meeting, "I'm Sandy, and I have an addiction." I felt like the weight of the world had been lifted. I was part of the human race at last.

The Twelve Steps

"The Twelve Steps are a group of principles, spiritual in their nature, which, if practiced as a way of life, can expel the obsession . . . and enable the sufferer to become happily and usefully whole."

—from the foreword of *The Twelve Steps And Twelve Traditions*[1]

Personal Action

1. We admitted we were powerless over fear/obsession/addiction, that our lives had become unmanageable.
2. Came to believe that a power greater than ourselves could restore us to sanity.
3. Made a decision to turn our will and our lives to the care of God as *we understood Him.*
4. Made a searching and fearless moral inventory of ourselves.
5. Admitted to God, to ourselves, and to another human being the exact nature of our wrongs.
6. Were entirely ready to have God remove all these defects of character.
7. Humbly asked him to remove our shortcomings.
8. Made a list of all persons we had harmed, and became willing to make amends to them all.
9. Made direct amends to such people whenever possible, except when to do so would injure them or others.
10. Continued to take personal inventory and when we were wrong promptly admitted it.
11. Sought through prayer and meditation to improve our conscious contact with God *as we understood Him,* praying only for knowledge of his will for us and the power to carry that out.
12. Having had a spiritual awakening as the result of these steps, we tried to carry this message to others, and to practice these principles in all our affairs.

---

[1] *Twelve Steps and Twelve Traditions* (New York, NY, Alcoholics Anonymous World Services,1981) page 15

Dig Deep in One Place

The Twelve Steps are adapted and reprinted with permission of Alcoholics Anonymous World Services, Inc. Permission to reprint and adapt the Twelve Steps of Alcoholics Anonymous does not mean that A.A. is affiliated with this program. A.A. is a program of recovery from alcoholism. Use of the Steps in connection with programs and activities which are patterned after A.A. but which address other problems does not imply otherwise.

CHAPTER SEVEN

Let's Start Digging, Bill—Steps 1-6

"Half measures won't give me half; half measures will give me nothing."
—Bill

Step One—"Acceptance"

What does, "We are powerless over our fear/obsession/addiction and our lives had become unmanageable," mean? "Remember," my unofficial sponsor said, "You did Step One before you got in recovery. You did it out there when you were running and gunning. You did it every time you indulged in your addiction to control your fear when you didn't want to. I'm just giving you some information and clarification about you and your obsession. When you indulge in your addiction, a craving develops. That can be physical like nicotine, heroin, or alcohol, or it can feel emotional/mental as in gambling, hoarding, or control. If you are willing to stop anything for a week, we have a really good chance of success. You are well on your way. Pay attention to where your obsession is located. The unmanageability is the result of the direction your thinking is pointing. At the end, your every waking moment was consumed with your obsession. You were immersed in the delusion, and the result was wrinkled cars, jail jumpsuits, and ruined relationships. Fighting against this double-edged sword of the physical and the mental is impossible without help. So you surrendered. You surrendered when you said okay to treatment in that cabin above Estes Park. You surrender every time you acknowledge your obsession."

Wow! This could work on anything! Wow! From drugs to chocolate cakes in the closet before breakfast, one-armed bandits, hoarding, sex, money, or rock 'n roll. Why wouldn't everyone do this?

She continued, "It didn't happen to you until you were crushed by a self-imposed crisis. You were the victim of a delusion, not denial. Delusion is a mental illness. You were incapable of seeing the seriousness of your condition. You were lying in the gutter looking down on everyone else. Until these stark facts were accepted, nothing could be done. To do Step One perfectly, don't put the substance in you or indulge in the behavior that causes the craving to develop."

Step Two—"Open-Mindedness"

I don't believe in God. "So what?" my sponsor said. Well, God doesn't believe in me. "No one cares. Let's go to a meeting." But don't you have to believe in God to do the Steps? "Who told you that? All that's asked of you is to stop saying no. You don't have to say yes to anything. Just stop saying no." Well it says, "Came to believe that a Power greater than ourselves could restore us to sanity." So that means God, right? "Good grief," she exclaimed, "Lack of power is your dilemma. You need to find a power greater than addiction that will solve your problem. That's what the Steps are all about. If you'll do them, you will recover and be given the power to help others." So, what's the power? "Why, it's the power to help others! Call it anything you like, but that's the power greater than obsession. But you have to do it. You've got to go, and if you go, what you need will come. I can't describe it, I can't explain it, but I can get you there.

"Step Two is about open-mindedness. An open mind is a mind with nothing in it. Your mind is full of noise—you know, all your old ideas. It's called the consciousness of your belief, and it was smeared all over you when you got here—a 285-pound sweaty pig of a man just inches from death. So, we have to change the direction of your thinking, and you can't do it with your mind. We have to do it with your actions. That's why those meetings, washing cups, and taking out the trash work. Instead of automatic negative thinking with a curious twist of the mind, let's take some positive action that will help someone else. This is a spiritual not a religious program; God is anything that keeps you sober. The emphasis is on seeing what you can bring."

This insanity thing is delightful! When I finally took a look at how much I indulged my addiction, it was clearly insane. Albert Einstein's well-known definition of insanity is doing the same thing over and over expecting different results. My idea of what is acceptable is totally different from that of the people around me. Ridicule and being found out is the problem, and if that hasn't happened yet, what's the problem?

Dig Deep in One Place

Step Three—"Willingness"

How come I never saw any of this before? My spiritual mentor explained, "Because you don't know you are asleep until you wake up. A whole set of circumstances all conspired to wake you up. Your physical condition and mental state, the intervention and the love of those friends, and then your willingness when it all came together. That willingness opened a door that you never knew was there. Now we need action, and this is where Step Three comes in. 'Made a decision to turn our will and our lives over to the care of God as *we understood him.*' The *Big Book* was written by white, Anglo-Saxon, middle-class, Protestant, American men in the mid-to late 1930s. They had no other way to put it. Thank God they added, 'As we understood him.' It opened the door for everyone to participate."

My spiritual guide continued, "So, let's boil it down to three questions: What's your will? What's your life? What is your decision? The first two questions are easy. Your will is your thinking, and your life is your actions. One good look in the mirror ought to tell you how well that was working out for you. I don't have to say a word—you tell me. I know, I know, it was the fault of your wife, it was the police, the traffic, the job, friends, anything but you, you poor victim. The only thing you are a victim of is the delusion that you can wrest satisfaction out of this world if only people would do what you want. Didn't work out very well, did it? The third question is entirely up to you. You can't go back because it will kill you, but to go on with the rest of the Steps is really scary. I suggest you go on with the work. The decision is yours.

"Saying a prayer might help. Let's try this one: 'Spiritual Principles, I offer myself to you, to build with me and to do with me as you will. Relieve me of the bondage of fear, that I may better do these Spiritual Principles. Take away my fears, that victory over them may bear witness to those I would help of your power, your love, and your way of life. May I do these Spiritual Principles always.'"

Step Four—"Honesty"

As we continued our work, my mentor said, "If your decision is to go on with the rest of the Steps, there is some instruction that goes with it. Go directly from here and buy two spiral notebooks, one eight and a half by eleven inches and the other pocketsize. You will need them to do the next step. Don't put this off. A huge part of a spiritual awakening is following instructions. You will not be told to do anything that will harm you or anything that I haven't done myself. Now, go get your notebooks!"

Do I have to talk to you about that Vaseline and leather thing I was into the other night? My sponsor explains, "Morals have very little to do with sex. Your morals are your beliefs. 'Made a searching and fearless moral inventory of ourselves,' means we are going to pull all that noise out of your head and find out what your beliefs are. We are going to find out what lie you have been basing your life on. The Twelve Steps are the greatest gift ever given to mankind. They are a recipe to a spiritual awakening. The Fourth Step is a written exercise that will show you what's been ruling your life. Most people don't know that they are hardwired for sex, security, and society; that they wake up horny, hungry, and wanting to be somebody in the eyes of their fellows. The addict/obsessive is an extreme example of these drives. You never hear about the fourth drive, the search for spirituality. This is the only one that will save you. There are just two choices: an addict's death or a spiritual life. The Steps are a shortcut to a spiritual life. What is the spiritual life? Helpfulness to others. The reason it happens so fast is because you have already done your pilgrimage. It took you thirty years to get here. It can take a Buddhist monk twenty years to find enlightenment, but in just a few months you will realize you are the author of the madness that is your life."

We laid out this format. It's four columns, and each has a heading. I opened my notebook with a page on the left and the page on the right. At the very top of each page, I wrote: "Thank you, Spiritual Principles, for making me open, honest, and willing. Thank you, Spiritual Principles, for the words." Two inches in from the left edge I drew a line straight down from the top. I did the same on the right-hand piece of paper. At the top of the first of those four columns I wrote, "I am resentful at:" I said to myself, "But I'm not resentful at anyone. I just hate the SOB!"

I put down any person, institution, or principle I was mad at. If it occurred to me, I put it down. The second heading is, "The Cause (of my resentment)." The only things that could cause a resentment were where I was hurt, threatened, or interfered with. Column 3 was called, "Affects my." Pride, security, sex relations, personal relations, ambitions, finances, and self-esteem are all manifestations of fear, and these are what had been affected. To conclude that others were wrong was as far as I ever got. What if I went further? What if I put down my mistakes, wrongs, blame, and fault? Well, let me see what this looks like. I was resentful at my mother-in-law because she was making the mortgage payments. What did that affect? Well, my pride, self-esteem, and even my sex relations with Sandy. And my mistake, blame, fault, and wrong? I didn't make the mortgage payments.

Step Five—"Love"

I was not sure if I liked this. I looked ahead, and sharing all this with someone else had never been considered. That's Step Five. Did I have to tell someone I stole a friend's drugs and then helped him look for them? Do you have any idea what that makes me look like? It makes me look like a liar, a cheat, and a thief! It makes me look like I'm full of pride and anger as a result of no self-esteem!

In amongst all this anger and resentment was the moment my relationship with the human race changed, the moment I had proof of my inadequacy. As I mentioned before, that moment was being naked for the first time in gym class with all the other guys at the start of seventh grade. It was cold, and I was a skinny little white kid with shriveled-up genitals and not a hair on my body from the eyebrows down. There stood Tom. He'd been held back *two* grades. His was hanging on the ground, and he was covered with hair. He looked at me and laughed. I would never measure up. I spent the rest of my life gathering evidence for that lie. It's called obsession. I would not be given a diploma for my victimhood, but I could use this as a springboard into a spiritual life.

Step Six—"Forgiveness"

"Were entirely ready to have God remove all these defects of character." I stirred the pond of my life, and all the crap came to the surface. Was I willing to take responsibility for what I'd found, that I was a liar, a cheat, and a thief? Defects of character is a bit of a misnomer. It's the human condition. Remember sex, security, and society? Knowing where the saber-toothed tiger lives, getting something to eat, and impregnating every woman on the planet. These instincts are out of date today. I'm not likely to freeze, starve, or be eaten, but there is no way to shut them off. If I am unaware of them, I am dumber than a toilet. A toilet has a shut-off valve; the instincts don't. More is not enough. This is where we separate the men from the boys.

Because I was on a spiritual journey, what I needed to see would be shown to me. Step Six is where it happens. It's like discovering there's been a moose in my living room for the last thirty years. How could I not see it? This moose snapped into focus one afternoon during a big fight with Sandy while in the midst of this Step. After smashing a chair, I stormed out of the house yelling at the top of my lungs. Into the woods I crashed, wearing only a pair of cut-off jeans. After about a mile, I ground to a halt, no shirt, no shoes, no money. I was never going back! Oh my God, here was the behavior I'd been doing all my adult life. In every argument with Sandy, I jumped up and down, yelled and screamed and broke stuff, and then stormed off and pouted. If I'm louder than you it makes me right. There was the moose exposed. I was full of pride and anger as a result of no self-esteem, and I'd just seen what that looked like. What a priceless gift. I saw myself with crystal clarity for the first time in my life.

CHAPTER EIGHT

Discovery of Denial, Sandy—Steps 1-6

"We don't know we are asleep until we wake up."
—Sandy

Step One—"Acceptance"

I began to look for a sponsor. A sponsor is a person who has experienced Steps and who is willing to help someone else through them. I talked to a woman who invited me to her house. I went, and we talked about everything except working the Steps or the problem. I left kind of disappointed. I was expecting some deep revelation or something.

The next sponsor actually talked a little about the program; she asked if I thought I had a problem.

I said, "I don't know. I guess maybe I do."

She said, "Okay," and we went on to Step Two. She asked, "Do you think there is a power greater than yourself?"

I replied, "Sure, I guess so."

And on to Step Three. "Are you willing to turn your life and your will over to the care of a Higher Power?"

I said, "Sure, okay, I guess I have to."

And then she said, "All right, go write a searching and fearless moral inventory."

There were no directions, no encouragement, no nothing. I was scared to death. "How can I do that?" I asked desperately.

"Oh, the directions are right there in the *Big Book*," was the answer. I was lost. I couldn't see any directions. Where?

I foundered for the next three months, getting more and more trapped by my resentments and fears. I was drowning in them. I figured out somewhat of a format, but the release just wasn't there. I was stuck in my resentments with no way to go beyond. This was made even worse by the fact that I was no longer indulging my addictions. I had no solution at all.

There was one woman I was afraid to ask to sponsor me. She really seemed to know the program. She had ten years of recovery in the program;

that seemed like forever to me. I thought she might call me on my stuff, "make" me talk, "make" me participate in meetings, and real hard stuff like that. I didn't think I had a bad enough problem for her, but she was very kind and continued to ask me how the Fourth Step was going and encouraging me to finish. I couldn't; I was stuck. One night I heard her talking about the "sunlight of the spirit" and how wonderful it was to work with others. I was suddenly possessed by the thought that if I didn't learn to give this away, "they" wouldn't let me stick around. (Thank God, this is *not* true.) I also overheard her saying to someone else that the way to go through the Steps again was to take another person through them. I hadn't even been through them once. What was I to do?

I walked up to her after the meeting and asked if she could or would teach me how to give this away and if she couldn't or didn't have time, then would she help me to find someone who could? She laughed and said, "I would be honored and proud to help you."

My new sponsor said, "Put that Fourth Step you've been working on away. We're going back to the beginning and find out where you belong." It didn't matter, but she said I needed to know why I wanted to do these things. Most humans will not even consider taking the actions required by the Steps unless they have to do so to save their lives. So even though I may not have reached a bottom of total and absolute despair, I had reached the "skid row of the soul." My miserable despair was enough for me. This was Step One, "I am powerless over my fear/obsession/addiction and my life is unmanageable by me."

I remember asking her what I could possibly do to repay her; I somehow wanted to pay for the time and wonderful help she was giving freely to me. She said, "The only thing I will ask of you is that you make at least one attempt to pass these truths on to others after we have finished." I promised that I would, not knowing really what it was that I was agreeing to.

As we went through the literature of the program, she gave me specific directions on what to read for each assignment. We would then discuss the assignment, paying particular attention to the feelings described, not the details.

Looking at the "Doctor's Opinion" in the *Big Book*, she pointed out to me the feelings of restlessness, irritability, and discontentment. Did I

Dig Deep in One Place

ever feel like that? Did I drink, use some other chemical, or create some kind of dramatic behavior to fix that problem? Did I like the effect of alcohol, drugs, and drama? I knew it was not good for me, but I was not as bad as others I saw around me. How the hell did I know? If I was drunk, high, or upset, my judgment was impaired. I was unable to tell the true from the false. My way of living seemed the only normal one to me.

As we read "Bill's Story," obviously I was not the same person as the New York stockbroker in the 1920s and '30s. That was my grandfather. How could I possibly feel the same way? Okay, so when did I discover alcohol? I remembered the time at the house party in England. I drank the whole bottle of vodka. I loved the feeling. It took me away, and despite the fact that others made fun of me, I felt a part of something. I couldn't wait to do it again. Did anyone ever say anything to me about my behavior? Well the kids on the bus whispered that I was a "lush," which caused me to get sneaky. A couple of my boyfriends hadn't liked how I behaved. No problem, that's okay. There's other fish in the sea, and I set out to find them. Did I ever find others like me, as Bill W. did when he took up golf? Yes! Theater people and artists were perfect. When was there any amount of trouble or disagreement, what was the first thing I thought of? Escape via the bottle, drug, or relationship, of course.

How about those binge mornings when I would lie there on the couch, my heart pounding, knowing that I was going to die this time, a terrible sense of impending doom upon me, only to arise in an hour to have another drink and snort of coke? I had my solution to fear, and I was determined that it was going to last for me. What about the self-pity I felt when I looked in the mirror? It was just another hopeless place to be. I needed to ask myself, "Do I really need to go to the bottom of the pit before I reach out for help?" Yeah, but you don't understand. "I can't ask for help. I'm supposed to be able take care of this myself." Remember, I wasn't supposed to get addicted to any of this stuff. Alcohol is my right as an adult American human being, and the other stuff is only psychologically addicting. I'm safe; I'm too smart and strong for that. Addiction creeps in and takes over without my permission but with my unconscious consent.

Okay, what about unmanageability? "Yeah, what about it?" It all came down to this overwhelming fear in my life. When I found alcohol, it took care of the fear for at least a little while. Drugs helped a little, and then relationships filled the rest. I thought I had found the solution to this problem of fear that started so early in my life. We moved every two years. I became shy, painfully shy. It was not only painful to me; it was painful to everyone around me. The self-consciousness and self-centeredness would absolutely paralyze me. Alcohol, drugs and relationships were my solutions to this feeling of fear, and I became determined that I could make these solutions work forever. They were a way for me to control and manage my fear. I am powerless over my fear. It had become impossible for me to manage my life to control the fear on my own. The alcohol was not working anymore. There was no one else who could save me, and I had no other tools. I must find another solution to this fear problem. This is called "acceptance" and is the realization that I have been avoiding the truth. I'd had a problem for a long time. It didn't matter that my sneakiness, control, hiding, and denial seemed to work for many years. They weren't working anymore. This was a self-imposed crisis I could no longer avoid or postpone.

Step Two—"Open-Mindedness"

So here's another new idea, "open-mindedness." I had made alcohol, drugs, and relationships my Higher Power. They did for me what I could not do for myself. They took care of the fear problem, made me social, and gave me courage, serenity, and what I thought was joy and happiness. How could there be anything more powerful than that? So it has to be a power greater than alcohol, drugs, or relationships to be my solution to fear.

And what is sanity? Maybe being unable or unwilling to practice the Spiritual Principles of acceptance, open-mindedness, willingness, honesty, love, forgiveness, truth, hope, light, etc., is insanity. While it was true that I had sometimes been able to practice these ideas, it was by accident rather than by design. I was often pleased with the results, but I could not repeat, because my actions were reactions to fear and not by choice.

I had already admitted in the First Step that I had been living in a world of delusion, that I could not tell the true from the false. Maybe I hadn't been truly sane for a long time. I had always been a seeker. I had looked at various religions; none spoke to me entirely or absolutely. I wanted a solution, but I had a lot of prejudice against what I perceived as churchy words such as thee, thou, etc. I believed I saw an attitude of righteous superiority in religious people. It had already had been suggested me to change the words in the prayers if I felt more comfortable with that. So I did that. I changed God to Spiritual Principles, Thee to you, and Wilt to will until it made sense to me.

In fact, it is repeated over and over in the literature of Twelve-Step programs that we can choose our own conception of a power greater than our fear, addiction, or problem. All that is asked of me is that I stop saying *no;* I do not have to say *yes* to anything or everything in the program. Just stop saying *no.* Well this is a step into open-mindedness. I could start with that! So I changed the words. I asked myself what the spiritual expressions really meant to me. These suggestions brought me to the conclusion that my old ideas and behaviors were not working. I might as well try something new and different.

I had been through my fling with atheism and had ended up miserable. Religion had never spoken to me, and my experience with prayer and spiritual solutions didn't seem to work. There seemed to be no place else to go. My solutions were no longer working. I had to turn to a power greater than my fear. Go ahead! It doesn't matter where you start; just start.

Step Three—"Willingness"

Now we moved to Step Three. I certainly understand a lot more than the first time I had attempted this process. This made much more sense. It was much more practical. This was something I could do.

"Okay." My sponsor said, "Now you get to make a decision to turn your will and your life over to this power." I wasn't at all sure this power existed. "That's fine" she said. "All it takes is willingness, a willingness to do something different than you've ever done. First of all, let's look at how you have been living your life and how well has that been working."

I protested, "But I never demand anything. I'm quiet and shy and do everything for everyone else."

So let's take an example. Have you ever been in a play? Do you remember that there was one person designated to direct it? And everyone agreed to this arrangement? What would have happened if one of the actors decided that it should be done her way? And what if she tried everything she could to achieve that end? She might be kind, loving, and gracious or might be arrogant and demanding, but still nothing suits her. Wouldn't that cause chaos in the company? Everyone might start demanding that it be his or her way or nothing. The play might not ever come to the stage—all this because it was forgotten that there is a director who can see the big picture, not just the narrow, selfish, individual needs. We all have instincts for sex, security, and society that demand to be heard, and didn't I just as selfishly try to manipulate this for me using whatever tools I have to achieve my goals of relationships, safety, and prestige? The answer turned out to be yes. It may not look like a demand on the surface, but it is a demand nonetheless. The results are predictable: confusion reigns for me and all who surround me.

As I considered these very unflattering truths—that I indeed had been selfish and self-centered, that shyness was actually a manifestation of self-centeredness and fear—I was beginning to see that I caused my own troubles more often than not. In my pursuit of protecting myself, to put the world into a box so I could feel safe, I had hurt and worried other people. My excuse was that I only did what I thought I saw others do to get what they wanted. In my world, this wasn't selfish. That's the way the world was, and besides, wasn't this a selfish program? My sponsor said, "Sure, the program is selfish in the fact that you must be willing to save yourself so that you can be helpful to someone else, but you must be free of this selfishness or it will kill you."

So how was this decision to be accomplished? What was it that I could do? Did I have to do something that was really difficult or hard to do? My sponsor replied, "No, just bring your willingness to say a prayer, to participate in a meeting, to ask for help, to make a phone call, to do the assignments you have been given, and to bring your enthusiasm to do these things. Take these actions and we have a real chance of changing your thoughts and attitudes." The decision comes up every day. Step Three is an ongoing practice. I am making a decision to pay attention to my thoughts, actions, and motives and take some deliberate action. Fear no longer has to be my employer.

What it really comes down to is that there is a Higher Power, and I am not it. I cannot control everything in my life in order to feel safe. I can call the Spiritual Principles anything I wish; the important thing is that I become an agent of those ideals. When I make an effort to understand and practice the principles in my life, I have made a decision to change.

Step Four—"Honesty"

I was back in Step Four. I really felt more prepared to take a fact-finding and fact-facing look at my life and myself. What a relief! Now I got out my notebook I had worked so hard on. It wasn't so bad. The format would actually work. I had taken a spiral notebook and opened it so there was a blank page on either side of the spiral. On the left side I drew a vertical line about two inches in from the edge. On the right side I made another vertical line about two inches in from the spiral to give me a small column and a wide column on each page. This gave me more space than any other configuration I had tried. I could see the whole thing at once without having to flip pages back and forth. On the far left side the name of the first column is "I'm resentful at." The second (wide) column is entitled, "The cause or what happened to piss me off." The third column is "Affects my." And the fourth (wide) column asks, "Where were my mistakes, fault, or blame?" At the top of each page is a spot for a prayer: "Thank you, God, for making me open, honest, and willing. Thank you, God, for the words" Nothing counts but thoroughness and honesty. Spelling and neatness do not count, if it occurs, I write it down, and if it doesn't occur, well, I don't write it down.

I had done quite well with the first two columns: Who am I resentful at? What happened to make me angry? They are pretty straightforward. Plenty of things had happened to me to be resentful, ranging from resentment against the U.S. Air Force because they didn't allow girls to become fighter pilots, to the double standard concerning marriage and relationships, personal hurts, and the institution of drinking. Sure I had plenty to be angry about, but here I was now still stuck in those things. The only difference now was that by understanding the first three steps, I was beginning to see there could possibly be a different way to deal with my anger and resentments. I was protected by a power greater than myself and my decision to go on with the rest of the work.

Anger could be defined as "fear announced," so it's all fear. Column three, "Affects my," is all about the seven main areas affected by this fear response.

1. Self-esteem—how I feel about myself.
2. Security—what I think I need to feel safe.
3. Ambitions—what I think I need to be happy.
4. Pride—how I think others see me.
5. Personal relationships—friends, coworkers, family, etc.
6. Intimate relationships—sex, marriage, and love.
7. Pocketbook—how much money will I have?

And all these come down to fear. If any of these things are hurt, threatened, or interfered with, they have been affected. This always results in fear. We could call it anxiety, stress, frustration, angst, or shyness. All these are fear, plain and simple, in the end. I ask myself these questions about each of my resentments that I have written down.

Now it was time to look at column four. Where had I been wrong? That is really baffling to me and the only one I hadn't done a thing on. Every time I thought about it, my brain seemed to turn to mush. Thoughts started whirling around. First I thought, *Well, it's all my fault. I am the worst.* Then came the thought *that it was all their fault.* I vaguely knew that none of this was entirely true. I was not the worst. I was not the best, but I was unable to stop the noise in my head. This was where my sponsor stepped in to stop the madness. She asked, "Where is the Higher Power in all this? Just write to the best of your ability and honestly what it is that you did wrong. Set aside all the other junk."

I took a look at this resentment: I believed my mother had always thought I made bad decisions. What did that affect? My self-esteem, my security, my pride, my ambitions, personal relationships, sex relationships, and my pocketbook. It all came down to fear. Where was I wrong? I refused to make decisions, or at best I waited until I was forced into a choice. I turned away and refused to forgive. I refused to be accepting, open-minded, and honest, so what it really looked like was that I was being sneaky and manipulative. Oh, if only I had been Bonnie and Clyde, it would have been so much easier to admit to big crimes against humanity, or so it seems. I didn't want to admit that I was small, so I told small lies because I just wanted to get by in life. I did the best I could to write down a all of this.

But this isn't all there is to an inventory. I did an inventory of all those other fears besides the ones I had already written down—just a simple list. Afraid of being alone, afraid of not being alone, fear of abandonment, fear of dying, fear of big dogs, fear of not being enough— ah! Doesn't it all come down to that! "I am not enough." It comes in all sorts of disguises, but there it is. Maybe the truth is that we are not enough, and that's okay! That's why we need the Spiritual Principles to guide us through to become the things we need to be. We can be the agents to produce these things: acceptance, open-mindedness, willingness, honesty, love, forgiveness, harmony, truth, faith, hope, light, and joy in this world.

Next is the sex inventory. No, it's not actually about the act of sex. It's about my attitudes and actions surrounding intimate relationships, whether there was any actual sex or not. So I wrote down a list of my relationships, starting with Tommy in the first grade, and asked myself these questions: Was I jealous and afraid? Was I dishonest or selfish? Did I hurt anyone? Where was I at fault? Should I or could I have done anything different? This was not for condemnation of this very important part of life but to take an honest look at my past actions as they had affected others and myself. This made it possible for me to make choices on how I would act and react in my present and future relationships.

Finally, I wrote an assets list, a list of things that were good about myself: I am creative, I am loving, I am forgiving, I have a sense of humor, I am a good teacher, I am patient, I am a good wife, I work hard, I am good sponsor, I take care of my health, and I have womanly thighs. So there you go.

Step Five—"Love"

I had written a lot more now, so we went on to Step Five, which is to discuss what I had written myself with another human being and with God. The terrible fear I had been feeling about actually sharing this with another human being was beginning to subside. Just writing it all down produced some results. The act of sharing is on the surface an act of confession, but for me it was much more than that. I became a part of the human race at last. I found that I was not the only person who had been selfish and self-centered, who wanted what she wanted now. The seeds of compassion that were planted in Step Four were beginning to sprout. Maybe other people had reacted out of fear. Maybe that's why they had behaved just as badly toward me. Maybe this was why they'd hurt me. Maybe they were infected just like me with the spiritual disease of fear. Could I be helpful? Would I forgive them? What a novel idea! I couldn't possibly be the only selfish person out there.

The real reason for telling someone else the exact nature of my wrongs becomes clearer as I do it. This is the first time the pattern of my life has been revealed. I have never before been able to put a finger on what was holding me back from being the person I knew I could be. The truth is that unless I can clearly see this, there is no chance I will be able to change my selfish behavior. To be able to see and accept who and what I really am without self-pity or pride allows the change.

A Memory

When I was around eight years old, I stole a quarter from a neighbor's mantle. I had no reason; I just wanted it. I knew it was wrong, but I when I was asked about it, I totally refused to admit I had done this. I knew they knew that I had stolen it, but I still stuck with my story. I hid the quarter away, never to spend it or enjoy it, and forgot about this incident for years. I suddenly remembered this while doing my Fifth Step. As I look back on it now, this was the moment my relationship with the world changed. Now I had something to hide, something that made me bad. This lie built a wall that separated me from everyone else. I believe this is where my shyness really started. I became afraid that you would find out that I had lied, that I was scared, that I was not enough. The realization dawned that I was indeed the author of my life, and I could no longer blame anyone else.

When we finally finished, my sponsor said, "Now go home, take a look at the work we have done so far, and ask yourself if you left anything out or if there is anything else that needs to be said."

This process of the Steps is actually very gentle, and I am led to see that what I need to see in increments. Step Five is the continuation of this process of humility that started in Step One to see what and who I really am, followed by a sincere attempt to become what I could be.

Step Six—"Compassion"

Let's move on to Step Six. My sponsor said, "I want you to read Step Six in the *Twelve Steps and Twelve Traditions* every day until we meet at our regular time next week." This was six days worth. As I read it the first time, I was unable to relate to the to the words or ideas; it was like Chinese to me. As I read it again and again, something started to happen—this was me! The information snuck past my left-brain that was irritated and slipped into my right brain. Step Six says: "Were entirely ready to have God remove all these defects of character." I needed to change that to, "Thank you, Spiritual Principles, for showing me what has been holding me back." So I was asking to be shown anything else in my thoughts or actions that were standing in the way of my being able to practice Spiritual Principles in my life.

Yeah, but defects of character sound like something really bad—something like sins that can never be forgiven, isn't that right? What if I think of sins as defined as "to miss the point"? Aren't defects a lot like that? Maybe I think I'm actually getting something from my defects or shortcomings. If I lie, cheat, or steal, it may look like I get something from it, but I'm missing the point, that it really is a spiritual law that I cannot enrich myself at the expense of another human being. Again, I do not want to admit that I have been sneaky and manipulative. What does that make me look like? I remember that in the past I made statements like, "You wouldn't like me if you knew who I really am." I had to keep my wall of isolation in place or my fear that you would know who I really was would ruin my control of the situation.

CHAPTER NINE

What Can I Bring?, Bill—Steps 7-12

"Knowledge is in your head;
understanding is in your heart."
—Bill

Step Seven—"Harmony"

Step Seven talks about humility. Just what is it? From the book *Twelve Steps and Twelve Traditions* comes the definition: "It amounts to a clear recognition of what and who we really are, followed by a sincere attempt to become we could be."[2] This is the flowering of compassion. The seedling that sprouted in Step Four when I learned that just maybe all these people on my list were perhaps spiritually sick like me. How could I judge anybody when I was a liar, cheat, and thief? Maybe we are *all* suffering from the human condition. Maybe making someone else's journey harder isn't a good idea. Indeed, the attainment of a clear recognition of what and who I really am, followed by a sincere attempt to become what I could be, is the foundation principle of each of the Twelve Steps. As I read Step Seven every day, just like Step Six, understanding starts to come. I always read for knowledge, but this was something different. By reading it for a week, my head stopped listening at four days, and my heart started to hear. Knowledge is in the past, the head. Understanding skips the head and lands in the heart. By substituting the definition for the word humility every time it appeared in the reading, there was no doubt what its wider meaning was. This was a little awkward, as the word humility appears twenty-five times in just seven pages. What could I be? Acceptance, open-mindedness, willingness, honesty, love, forgiveness, harmony, truth, faith, hope, light, and joy will do for a start.

Here's a story that skips the head. Rounding the corner of a ruined building three days after Hurricane Katrina somewhere between Biloxi and Baton Rouge, a TV news crew spots a woman sweeping Interstate 10. Approaching her, they ask, "Do you live around here?" She points

---

[2] *Twelve Steps and Twelve Traditions*, (New York, NY, Alcoholics Anonymous World Services, Inc. 1981) page 58

and the camera pans slowly; nothing but destruction. Even the trees are smashed. Back to her, she says, "I've always wondered what it would be like to have nothing. Now I know. But this morning I found this brand-new broom, and God said time to get busy. So, if you'll excuse me, I've got some sweeping to do." Every once in a while you get to meet an angel.

Step Eight—"Truth"

The list of people I have harmed started to make sense. This was obviously going to be a great relief in my life, but it was not about me. It was about cutting the chains that bound these people to me. It was really about setting *them* free! I was now in a position to offer them a piece of sacred ground to stand on, a place for them to let their fears fall from them. Because I was in this place, anyone who occurred to me had to go on the list. There were even people I had never harmed, but I was asked to offer them the keys to the kingdom also. Holy cow! A way to change the past! My past was becoming the greatest asset I had. No one gets into heaven carrying a bag of trash. This was where I put the garbage down. It was going to require a couple of different kinds of letters. I noticed I couldn't change my thinking with the mind I showed up with. I had to change my actions; the whole first part of this program is about action, action, and action. First I wrote a forgiveness letter to myself. Forgiveness does not mean to condone; it means to cease to resent. I wrote to myself:

> *Dear Bill,*
>
> *I forgive you for being human. (Here I allow a higher power to speak to me and fill this in with a few details—no negativity, only gratitude. This was not to beat myself up but to grow in understanding.)*
>
> *God bless you,*
> *I love you,*
> *Bill*

I know this is the whole letter, but somehow it doesn't seem to be enough. Okay, here is the birth of the gratitude letter. Put only positive things in it. Nothing negative allowed, like, thank you, Spiritual Principles for a real way out, the solution to any difficulty that enters my life. Thank you, Spiritual Principles, for my awesome sponsor, teacher, and guide. Thank you, Spiritual Principles, for the Twelve Steps. I'd never done anything like this before. It was a wholesale change in my attitude and outlook on life.

This was the first genuine expression of my gratitude; it opened my heart so I would have the words when the time presented itself to be of help—help for anyone who asks.

Step Nine—"Faith"

Now a second letter; this one was to everyone else. This prayer went on the top of this page, like every other piece of paper I have touched in this process: "Thank you, Spiritual Principles, for making me open honest and willing. Thank you for the words."

> *Dear . . .*
> *I owe you an amend.*
> *Today I am living a spiritual life, and part of the program of recovery for freedom from alcohol is restitution for harm done.*
> *I was wrong to have harmed you by my (thoughts, words, actions). A short explanation of what it was.*
> *I deeply regret having done this.*
> *Is there anything else I can do to make this right?*
> *Is there anything you would like to say?*
> *God bless you,*
> *I love you, Bill*

I kept what I did short, sweet, and to the point because it was about opening the doors of paradise for them. It was about swinging wide the gates of heaven. It was about lifting the hatch to let the sunlight of the spirit in. I did this open the door for them three times. I was wrong. Is there anything else I can do to make this right? Is there anything you would like to say? Their response made no difference because I didn't know what their fear looked like.

I used this format for every one of my amends. The letter clarified in my mind the amends and helped keep it very simple. In most every case the amends were done in person. In the one to my friend, I said, "I was wrong to have stolen your dope and help you look for it." He was in a hospice at the time looking like a ninety-year-old man bleeding from his ears, eyes, and feet. "Don't touch any fluids!" said the nurse. He died shortly after of drug and alcohol abuse. In lieu of paying him, we made a donation to the hospice.

The amend to my mother-in-law was, "I was wrong to have not made the mortgage payments." We owed her thousands. Sandy and I made an appointment with her to make the amends in a just-opened Mexican restaurant. New waiters and bus boys were being trained, and the place was full of diners. Perfect; she wouldn't be able to hear a word. It was so loud; ear damage was a real possibility. I opened my mouth to start, and like an episode of *Star Trek,* a bell jar came down around us. Time froze, and nobody moved. Out poured the amend as we all held hands. We came prepared to make payments, but she forgave the debt, saying she had helped out the other siblings with a similar amount. As we released our hands, the bell jar disappeared and the noise returned. Instead of a person I feared and hated, I now have a real friend.

The amend to my dad took a year and a half till I could get back to Minnesota to tell him I'd stolen his paintings. I sold or traded them for money to indulge my obsession. I thought he didn't notice. If a piece of my art went missing wouldn't I know? But what *had* bothered him was me calling him while dead drunk when he was in the hospital with prostate cancer. I don't remember one single call; I was in a blackout. So I just listened to him talk. From that day I called him every Sunday morning to tell them I loved him. About four months before he died in 2005, he started to tell me he loved me back. It took me about nine years to finish all the amends I'm consciously aware of because every time I got a protégé to Step Nine, a new one would crop up. It reached the point where I was going to stop sponsoring people! The one thing that was really noticeable was that not one of them came out the way I thought it would. Nine times out of ten the unexpected happens.

Dig Deep in One Place

Step Ten—"Hope"

I had been living in a junkyard and didn't even know it. What's one more old hubcap when you're surrounded by wrecked cars, useless old appliances, and trash? In Steps Four through Nine, enough junk was cleared away to catch a glimpse of the horizon. Wow, there might be a sunset or even a rainbow! How wonderful! It was going to take persistent action to clear away all of that, but now I could see why the effort is worth it. Step Ten was essential to keeping the garbage from creeping back. It states I should "continue to take personal inventory and when I am wrong promptly admit it." Thank God there are sponsors to guide a person through this process, and I found a man who had been taken through the Steps. Howard was his name, and when he moved away, it was only to Denver! I called him every Wednesday at 5:30 for eight and a half years until he was killed riding his bicycle on Colorado Boulevard during rush hour. Ouch! He was run over by a seventeen-year-old drunk driver.

Step Ten asks that I watch for the re-emergence of my addiction. Every time it's the lie, I'm not good enough or I'm inadequate. The lie looks like a disturbance. It's a spiritual truth that every time I am disturbed there is something wrong with me. The disturbance is a red flag. It doesn't matter if it comes as selfishness, dishonesty, resentment, or fear. In my case, the alcoholism returns as the pattern I discovered in Steps Four and Five. I yell, break things, and pout. One of the greatest breakthroughs in my recovery happened as a Tenth Step. After an argument with Sandy one afternoon, I went off across the valley from our house and into the woods for a walk. Standing alone and still seething with anger, I watched as Sandy returned from the store and parked near the house. I was planning to shout my displeasure at her when I looked down. It had snowed about six inches the night before, and I was standing dead center in the wing prints of an eagle. The anger ran out of me, and I was filled with wonder. My God! I have a choice about how I behave today. I yelled at Sandy, but this time with excitement: "Come quickly, you have to see this!"

Everything changed. Instead of an uptight, seething week of silence, we had an awesome afternoon of productivity and joy. That's Step Ten in action. Which would I rather have, terror, bewilderment, frustration, and despair or happy, joyous freedom? It doesn't seem like a very hard choice, but before these Twelve Steps, I didn't even know there was a choice, and if I did, I would have asked what the third one was. Do no more harm. The best way to do that is the most powerfully practical Spiritual Principle of all: *shut up!* "But I have something to say." Yeah, we know, just shut up. Ninety percent of all my problems disappear when I just shut up.

Step Eleven—"Light"

You can only harvest what you plant. If you plant corn, no matter how much you wish, hope, and pray, cotton isn't going to come up. It's like an argument with gravity; I'm not going to win. My thinking is my prayer and all prayers are answered. If my thinking is negative, that's what comes. Planting fear makes fear the harvest. Step Eleven states, "Sought through prayer and meditation to improve our conscious contact with God as we understood him, praying only for knowledge of his will for us and the power to carry that out." I no longer want fear as my god. The harvest was unbearable, but I could not change it until I saw it. My prayer is my thinking, my meditation is my action, and the result is my life.

I spent most of my life worshiping fear and being a slave to the human condition, so practicing a spiritual life was awkward and new to me. If I wanted love, light, and joy to be my god, it was going to take my participation and persistence. The struggle was against forty-six years of bad habits and three million years of instinct. What I did now would set the pattern for the rest of my life. Instead of taking, instead of helping myself, let's see what I could bring. What is a spiritual life? It's helpfulness to others.

There are some really practical, seemingly insignificant things I can do. I can be a gift to every person I encounter today. I can give him or her a compliment or a blessing. I can tell the person behind the counter that his or her smile lights up the room. I can make some cards with the Spiritual Principles on them and hand those out everywhere. I can give one to the guy holding a sign on the street corner along with a dollar and tell him I love him.Yeah, but he'll just spend it on_____. Shut up! My judgment isn't asked for. I have two feet; he doesn't have any. My judgment is the chief block to a spiritual life. Acts of kindness make me feel physically better. I'm sure there is a scientific explanation for this. An act of kindness makes the receiver of it feel better. Anyone observing this act of kindness feels better. Everybody wins.

There are lots of kinds of meditation, and many of them involve action: tai chi, tae kwon do, karate, yoga, working out, creating art, working, running, or walking. I'm amazed that answers to questions I have about actions to take come during my morning workout. The first time this happened, I stopped and ran over to the table to write it down. "Why do you think you're going to forget the voice of the Universe?" Sandy asked. She was right. I've never forgotten. We also sit quietly for ten minutes or so. In my case it is not to quiet my mind, because restlessness seems to be its very nature, but to just observe the thoughts as they pass by. By observing them, I become used to what they look like. It's like a train yard. I don't have to get on board that outbound train. I don't have to make a nest for and feed these thoughts. Just because I have them doesn't make them true or right. In the past, I had no choice but to get on board and go. Today with an act of my own will I can point my thoughts, my prayers, in any direction I wish and follow them up with affirmative action. Being eleven steps up off the train yard, I have a better view. I can see those trains a-comin'!

Step Twelve—"Joy"

I may have made it to the starting gate! Step Twelve says, "Having had a spiritual awakening as the result of these steps we tried to carry this message to alcoholics and practice these principles in all our affairs." How the spiritual awakening happened is fascinating. It started with the surrender and some information about alcoholism I didn't have. My life was really a mess, and I needed some help. Asking for help is virtually impossible for an addict. The only power that will help is a spiritual life, and the shortcut to that life is helpfulness to others—real help, not jobs, food, clothing, money, shelter, a new truck, and a babe but the way to solve any problem that will enter my or anyone else's life. With this look at what my thinking and actions had done, I made the decision to continue with this program. Emptying the noise in my head with the help of another person was one of the most remarkable things I have ever done. There wasn't room for anything but darkness. I felt I would float off. Now there was room for something positive. There was also room to see what had been holding me back. I had to stop acting like a baby. "I want my way! I am never wrong!" It was embarrassing. The whining was over. How could I judge you when I was you! We all need a hand to get out of the ditch. With my list, I knew what needed to go to the dump. My amends are not done until I finish them all. Half measures will not do. I must finish my apprenticeship, setting all these people free.

I am now prepared to help any human being on the planet. The reason I am asked to specifically work with addiction is because no one else can. The judge can't help, nor can the police, and I don't know of one obsessive who asked for help because their mother wanted them to. Keep an eye out for the obsession moving up from the back row. It's very sneaky and powerful. It's as cunning as a wounded water buffalo. Anything that isn't the Spiritual Principles is the obsession. The thing that helps the most is helping someone else. My thinking and actions stay pointed in the right direction. The greatest gift of all is that I don't get a day off. Every day is a day I must do this. What a joy! Anybody can get to this awakening because there is a recipe: practice, practice, practice. That's another reason to go to those meetings. That's where I practice. Out in the world it's always game time! Thank God I am now prepared.

CHAPTER TEN

Faith is Action, Sandy—Steps 7-12

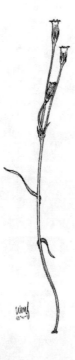

"Forgiveness simply means to cease to resent."

"A good definition for acceptance is to joyfully and willingly receive that which is presented."
—Sandy

Step Seven—"Responsibility"

If Step Six is asking to be shown what has been holding me back, then Step Seven is all about taking responsibility for who and what I have been in my life. This is not to beat myself up—oh no. I spent far too many hours doing that in the past. How can this be different? First, I don't like the way it's written. Step Six says, "Humbly asked him to remove my shortcomings." There has got to be a better way to put it. This sounds like wimpy religious stuff, and the word *humbly* reminds me of Uriah Heep in David Copperfield. If that's what being humble means, I want nothing to do with it!

Did this mean I couldn't do Step Seven? Was I stuck here now and forever? My mentor said, "Well, I don't think so. What is the one character defect that seems to cause you the most trouble?"

I thought and replied, "Refusal to take responsibility; what does that have to do with Step Seven?" It had come up over and over, and now it was even more apparent that it didn't work. So in Step Seven, we take responsibility for who and what we have been in our lives. Instead of trying to hide, I was being asked to acknowledge and accept the mistakes I'd made in the past. This was not to beat myself up but to build self-esteem. It's amazing, every time I do this, there is relief. Who knew that this was the way to freedom of the human spirit, the way to self-esteem? If I want self-esteem, I must do something that builds self-esteem. This was something I had missed. When I stole that quarter, it seemed to confirm that I was bad. This may have been true, but it was the relentless campaign where I gathered evidence for my low opinion of myself that did the most damage. It built the wall between me and the world. This low opinion provided me with all sorts of reasons and justifications for my actions. I was getting something from this—a reason for self-indulgent behavior. I didn't really need an excuse, but it sure was good to have one.

I was now discovering that there was a profoundly lazy part of myself. I liked the ease of the solution of alcohol, drugs, and relationships. It was like magic—it worked. It changed my outlook and attitude instantaneously without much effort on my part beyond supplying myself these substances. There is still that lazy part of me. It doesn't want any pain; it wants instant results. It doesn't want to think, take responsibility, or do anything that builds self-esteem. It wants instant sainthood, but it doesn't want to be bored either. I remember that I became an artist because I loved living on the edge. I chose this lifestyle because I loved the uncertainty.

Step Eight—"Forgiveness"

The seeds of compassion that were planted in Steps Four and Five sprouted in Steps Six and Seven and became seedlings. I needed to go on. Step Eight is suggesting that all-around forgiveness might be possible. This seemed highly improbable to me. I mean, aren't there some things that are unforgivable? What about the things have that have hurt me? What about the bad things and mistakes I made? My sponsor said, "I want you to write a forgiveness letter to yourself." I burst into tears. *This is impossible*, I think to myself, but how can I forgive anyone else if I cannot forgive myself? It's just too easy for me to rationalize my behavior with: "Sure, I hurt you, but really if you hadn't done what you did, I wouldn't have had to do what I did to you. Therefore, you owe *me* forgiveness."

I had to make an effort to do this. My letter read:

Dear Sandy,

> *I forgive you for being a human being. I forgive you for wanting what you wanted now. I forgive you for your fear and uncertainty that made you abuse and terrify a young girl who could not live up to your expectations. I am grateful that I have found a way to release you from your bondage of selfish fear to become a part of the human race. There were times I felt as though I was standing outside of the cage that we had built from shame, fear, envy, and resentment with a*

whip and chair saying, "Don't you dare to be free!" Today we have a way out. All we have to do is to practice the Spiritual Principles and help others—not very much really to experience happy, joyous freedom. So, Sandy, I bless the little girl who didn't know any better. We have a solution.

God Bless you, I love you,
Sandy

But this was only a part of Step Eight. I was given a list by the Universe of people who to some extent had been affected by my fear and bad behaviors. So this was my amends list, but it looked to me like I hadn't actually done anything to some of these folks. Why were they on this list? My sponsor said, "They are there for a reason or they wouldn't have appeared here. Let's explore this further. Maybe this list is all about giving a gift of forgiveness, to let them see what it is like to stand in the sunlight of the spirit, to give them the gift of acknowledgment of their hurts. You need to remember that no human wants to do this unless we have learned the great benefits of doing so. Not one person I know wants to stand up in front of another person and say I was wrong."

Step Eight says, "Made a list of all persons we had harmed and became willing to make amends to them all." So to become willing is the crux of this Step. First I forgive myself and then I am able to consider going to another and actually taking responsibility for myself and my past behavior.

Step Nine—"Truth"

This brings me to Step Nine, which says, "Made direct amends wherever possible except when to do so would injure them or others." This thing was starting to look different than it first appeared. I'd been thinking that it was going to be saying I was sorry, again. I had said I was sorry about a million times, it seemed. But that was all about getting caught. I have to say I'm sorry or you wouldn't leave me alone. I didn't mean it. I was sorrier that I had gotten caught or that you had noticed; there was no real remorse for wrongdoing or insensitivity on my part.

My sponsor suggested that I write a letter for each amend that appeared on my list. This was a continuation of the process of becoming willing to make amends. This letter needed to contain certain elements to help me keep this short and sweet, to help me not start to blame the other person or point out his or her faults. I was to stick to my wrongs, to sweep off my side of the street, so to speak. I was not to beg for forgiveness but to state where I had been at fault or had failed to practice the Spiritual Principles. Then I was to state my sincere regret (never saying I'm sorry) and desire to set right the wrong. I could ask three questions: 1. Is there any other way I may have harmed you? 2. Is there anything else I can do to make this right? 3. Is there anything you would like to say to me? Then at the end of the letter, I was to state my sincere desire not to repeat this behavior, bless them, wish them well, and give them my love.

My first draft of these letters really showed me where I wanted to blame everyone else. As we went over them, we culled any passages that contained blame or "Yeah, but . . ." and I was left with an amend I really felt I meant and could actually do. As I went out into the world to approach the people I had harmed, I found that most of the time what I imagined would happen didn't. The relief I felt was incredible. It felt like a miracle to actually and literally take responsibility for my past actions and myself. I did not have to hide the truth any more. The walls I had built with my lies were crumbling, and I began to take my place in the human race.

In Steps One through Nine I had, with a great deal of help, taken actions that I would never have dreamed of taking before being introduced to the Twelve Steps. These actions changed me profoundly. I had now examined many attitudes and motives that were part of my paradigm, the place I look at the world from, but I had never examined before. I had always just reacted to those motives and attitudes with no conscious thought. There were no choices—just reactions. Now after the work I'd done, I could actually start to make choices.

Step Ten—"Harmony"

All of this was preparing me to start to live a spiritual life. Step Ten reminded me to practice all of the first Nine Steps so I might maintain emotional sobriety and help others to do the same; in other words, to be a bringer of harmony rather than confusion and fear.

As I continued to do my amends, I was stepping into the sunlight of the spirit. The adventure of the first Nine Steps was like going deep into the dark forest of my soul. I had emerged into the sunlight again with a new understanding of myself. Now I had a way to deal with the fear in my life: practice the Steps and learn more about the Spiritual Principles.

Step Ten says, "Continued to take personal inventory and when we were wrong promptly admitted it." It assumes that I accept Steps One, Two, and Three. Step One is that there are many things beyond my control and I cannot manage them myself. Step Two is there might be a Higher Power that could help me. And Step Three is that I will make the decision to practice the principles and actions of Steps Four through Nine. This is especially important because life continues, I do wrong things, others do wrong or hurtful things, and accidents happen.

The whining is over. Step Ten tells me to do it or don't but quit whining about life. Shut up—it's me who has to shut up. It really doesn't matter what anyone else says or does. What is my response? That's the most important thing. Will I practice the Spiritual Principles? If I am disturbed, there something wrong with me. What is wrong with me? I am angry, fearful, envious, resentful, or upset. It's not that I'm in the wrong about some detail of the situation. Step Ten is all about humility, that clear recognition of who and what we really are. This works on the small and big things that happen.

A case in point: On a trip to New York City with Bill, I purchased a laptop computer for $800 more than it was worth. I overestimated my skills as a negotiator and got bamboozled. We were unable to get our money back, and when we got back to Denver, I was unable to forgive myself. The thoughts of, *I have made a terrible mistake, I'm stupid, and I wasted our money* became obsessive and impossible to control by myself. Despite reassurances from Bill that it was okay, that he wasn't upset, the money didn't matter and that he loved me, I continued on my path of self-pity and destruction. It was suggested that I engage in a written Tenth Step. At first I resisted, but it did offer a way out of my dilemma. Out came my notebook for a personal inventory of the situation, and in the process came relief.

As I wrote, I could see where I was at fault. I had walked into a store and put myself in a vulnerable position. I was such an easy mark; it must've been irresistible to the salesman. I was resentful at him for taking advantage of me. I was resentful at myself. *How could I have been so stupid?* This was my overriding thought. How could I forgive myself? I had to find a way. Resentment does not know who it belongs to, and it was spilling out all over my life again. Resentment lashes out at everyone around me and hurts myself and anyone else who happens to be around. A good definition for forgiveness is to cease to resent. There are no justified resentments. The damage I do to myself by drinking the poison of resentment eats me from the inside out. I found it was fairly easy to cease to resent the salesman. He will pay the price for his dishonesty, and he has to face the consequences of his actions just as I do mine. I do not have to damage myself with these thoughts. They don't hurt him, and only my soul is damaged. Did I owe him an amend? Probably not, but I did owe myself an amend. I did this by ceasing to resent. I shared all this with a confidant in the program so I could get a fresh view of the situation. So in all, I had now done Steps One through Nine again.

Deliberately going through this process again opens to the door to the solution every time. It's only my resistance that takes the time.

Step Eleven—"Faith"

I had always been a seeker. When I found my solution in alcohol and drugs, I thought my search was over, but it couldn't continue to work forever and it didn't. I had looked at various religions and spiritual paths, but none really spoke to me; I felt I was already too bad to be helped. When my self-imposed crisis brought me to the Twelve Steps, something started to make sense. Spirituality didn't have to be the dogma of a religion. Religion has to be in a box—they must define and refine their particular view of God and the world. There is nothing wrong with this; it just didn't work for me.

I had looked at the Golden Rule and thought it was a good idea but didn't seem to produce results for me. As it turns out, I had misunderstood the basic premise. Instead of "Do unto others as you would have them do unto you," I had interpreted it as saying: "I'll do unto you if you do unto me as I wish." I was the holder of the rules, which I could change without notice. Not surprisingly, it didn't work for them or me! The same went for other spiritual axioms. My interpretation was skewed just enough to guarantee failure.

The Twelve Steps asked me to seek to understand and practice the Spiritual Principles in my life. I could call them anything I wished just so long as I did them to the best of my understanding at the time and in all the situations in my life. Step Eleven encouraged me to use my interests to pursue knowledge of the principles in any direction I liked, provided I brought this information back to the program to help others as my experience, to bring strength and hope to others.

I had been learning through the actions called for in the previous Steps to pray and meditate. Each Step asked me to take this a little further. Now I was asked to focus on the practice. There are many kinds of meditation. One example is to read and concentrate on a particular idea or prayer, to relax, give up my arguments, and reflect on the truths written by someone else or even myself. I then asked what these ideas meant to me, to envision what it might look like in my life if I were able to practice the truth instead of believing the lie I have always assumed to be true.

There are many forms and practices of meditation. To sit and contemplate is one, but there are also acts of creativity, such as writing or painting, yoga practices of all kinds, and physical movement, including exercise, walking, running, or dancing. The list is endless. I have learned that the infinite possibilities are without boundaries and I am free to follow my interests.

Then there is prayer—what kind works? I have been told many times in the Steps that a self-serving demand for my selfish ends does not work. I have found through practice that this is true. My either/or prayers are useless. I feel like a little kid saying to Santa Claus, "Okay, fork over the pony or else!"

"Or else what?"

"I won't believe in you!" How ridiculous, but that's the form so many of my prayers have taken in the past. What if I ask, "What is God's will for me today?" and do the next loving thing, not necessarily the next right thing, although they could be the same? What if I pray for the abundance of God's will, the Spiritual Principles, in someone else's life? That means I've taken the selfishness out of the prayer that the other person get better so his or her behavior won't bother me anymore.

There are times when circumstances, sheer resistance, and the spiritual disease of fear seem to conspire to stop me from meditation and prayer. I may be vulnerable for many different reasons. Maybe I'm physically healing, or perhaps life hands me a gift that is wrapped in barbed wire I don't feel prepared to face. The question is then, do I have or can I find the faith and resources to meet these challenges? Occasionally I may be so resistant that I absolutely refuse to pray or meditate. What then? I need to continue to make the next best choice until I can reconnect, without spending extra time and abusing myself for my failure, because that just keeps me isolated within me, myself, and I. That does no good for me or anyone around me. I am incapable of being useful or practicing the Spiritual Principles in this state of mind.

My conclusion has to be that practice and persistence in Step Eleven works in my daily life.

Step Twelve—"Hope"

Finally I was at Step Twelve. I couldn't believe it. Step Twelve has three parts. The first is, "Having had a spiritual awakening as the result of these steps." As I look back over this journey, I am amazed! My attitude and outlook on life changed radically. I was still the same person, my circumstances had not changed, and yet everything had changed for the better.

What is a spiritual awakening? Well the first thing I knew was I had not arrived anywhere. I had just awakened as in after a long sleep. I didn't know I'd been asleep until after I woke up. This is what this feels like. Everything has a clarity, a newness, and a translucence. Everything is okay, everything is just as it should be, and I am as I should be! Yet I know I'm only at the beginning of learning this new life. An awakening! I made myself ready through the process of the actions of the Steps to receive this gift of awareness. It appears that a spiritual life is becoming aware of who and what I really am, my motives and attitudes, with a sincere desire to reach for the Spiritual Principles embodied in the Twelve Steps. But this is still just the beginning of the great adventure, which continues to this day.

"Light"

The second part of Step Twelve says, "We tried to carry this message to others." I remember when I asked my new sponsor in the beginning, "Is there anything I can do to repay you?" I wanted to pay for what I was about to receive because if I paid for it, I would not have to be responsible for any part in the process beyond paying for it. This was all unconscious, of course. I had never actually been able to change my thinking in the past either, so I remained without a solution no matter how much I paid for it.

Her response to me was, "The only way to repay me is to make at least one attempt to give what I have given to you to another person." I agreed to do just that with enthusiasm, but when I agreed to this, I had no idea just what I was setting myself up for. Helping another to walk the path of the Twelve Steps is a bittersweet endeavor. It is the great adventure. Every single person I have attempted to help has given me a part of themselves. They are me, and I am them. Whether or not they actually go on to recover and help others is not the point. My job is to be prepared to pass on these eternal truths.

I am here to produce another sponsor. When I make a commitment to help another human being who doesn't know there is a way out, I am making a commitment to be there with a spiritual solution. It doesn't matter if I'm feeling well or even spiritual at that moment in time. In this way I help myself as well as the other. I help myself to remember the practice of the principles in my own life.

"Joy"

The third part of Step Twelve is, "And to practice these principles in all our affairs." This brings me full circle—right back to Step One to utilize all the Steps in conduct of my life today. This means with my family, friends, coworkers, and fellow travelers on the highway. This is the great adventure! It really doesn't matter what anyone else says or does; it matters how I respond to the life situations around me. I don't have to react out of fear. Today I have a choice; I can respond. And what happens if I make a mistake? What if I fail to do the next loving thing? My spiritual advisor says, "Choose again!" I get to choose again! I have a way to admit when I am wrong and ask for a second chance.

Right here, up pops that lazy part of myself whining once again, "Why does it always have to be me? Why do I have to practice these Spiritual Principles all the time? I don't want to have to think all the time!" Ah, it's still there! I have four basic instincts: sex, security, society, and the search for the spiritual. The first three are always clamoring for more, more, more. They are up before me in the morning with all kinds of selfish schemes and ideas for revenge. The only one I have to work for is the practice of the spiritual, which seems eminently unfair to my ego. I am looking for spiritual progress, not spiritual perfection. I reach for the seemingly unattainable by practicing day in and day out. In this way I have a chance to live a life that is full of self-esteem, and the by-product of that is happy, joyous freedom.

PART THREE

What It's like Now

"No action is ever lost. Nothing we do is without result"
—Bill

CHAPTER ELEVEN

Let's Dig Deeper—The Twelve Traditions

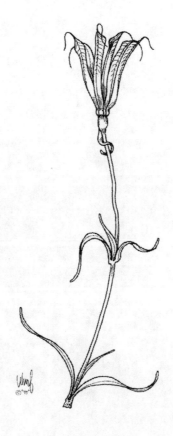

"If we will go, what we need will come"
—Bill

The Twelve Traditions

"The Twelve Traditions apply to the life of the fellowship itself. They outline the means by which the (group) maintains its unity and relates itself to the world around it, the way it lives and grows."
—from *The Twelve Steps and Twelve Traditions*[3]

Non-Action

1. Our common welfare should come first; personal recovery depends on Fellowship unity.
2. For our group purpose there is but one ultimate authority—a loving God as He may express himself in our group conscience. Our leaders are but trusted servants; they do not govern.
3. The requirement for membership is a desire to stop the obsession.
4. Each group should be autonomous except in matters affecting other groups or the Fellowship as a whole.
5. Each group has but one primary purpose—to carry its message to the individual who still suffers.
6. The Fellowship group ought never endorse, finance or lend the Fellowship name to any related facility or outside enterprise, lest problems of money, property and prestige divert us from our primary purpose.
7. Every group ought to be fully self-supporting declining outside contributions.
8. The Fellowship should remain forever nonprofessional, but our service centers may employ special workers.

---

[3] *Twelve Steps and Twelve Traditions*, (New York, NY, Alcoholics Anonymous World Services, Inc. 1981) page 15

9. The Fellowship, as such, ought never be organized; but we may create service boards or committees directly responsible to those they serve.
10. The Fellowship has no opinion on outside issues; hence the Fellowship's name ought never be drawn into public controversy
11. Our public relations policy is based on attraction rather than promotion; we need always maintain personal anonymity at the level of press, radio and film.
12. Anonymity is the spiritual foundation of all our traditions, ever reminding us to place principles before personalities.

The Twelve Traditions are adapted and reprinted with permission of Alcoholics Anonymous World Services, Inc. Permission to reprint and adapt the Twelve Traditions of Alcoholics Anonymous does not mean that A.A. is affiliated with this program. A.A. is a program of recovery from alcoholism. Use of the Traditions in connection with programs and activities which are patterned after A.A. but which address other problems does not imply otherwise.

Introduction to the Traditions

Now that we have had a real good look at ourselves and how we relate to the world around us, how can we put these spiritual principles into action? The Traditions developed by Twelve-Step fellowships can do just that. The Steps are personal actions that have saved our lives; the Traditions are twelve guidelines for the unity and conduct of recovery groups using the Twelve Steps. The Traditions, just like the Steps, start with a statement of the problem, followed by a statement of the solution. For example, the First Tradition asks the question, "How do we stay united as individuals for the good of the group because most individuals need the group for recovery?" The Second Tradition states the solution: Instead of a single leader we will listen to the group thought (conscious) as guided by a Higher Power or if you like, the Spiritual Principles. The rest of the Traditions deal with the specifics of putting the first two ideas into action. The Traditions show us exactly how much judgment we have in our lives.

We are going to be asked to connect; we must participate and at the same time withdraw from the contests that produce stress in our lives. This is the great adventure. We have found that these principles can be used in our daily lives to make a more harmonious world for everyone.

Tradition One—"Unity"

Living a spiritual life means we must keep these principles in the forefront of our minds. Why? Because we are constantly diverted. This is the First Tradition for everyone in recovery; it is our unity. It is for our common welfare. Without the life raft of the Steps, we all drown in the ocean of our own madness, whatever that may be. It may be sex, food, drugs, work, relationships, gambling, or alcohol. No matter what fights for your attention, return to the Steps. Return to the solution. Only individuals can do this, but we can't do it alone. This is a paradox. There is only one hole in the net that traps us. There is only one door in the prison that holds us. It's our connection with others. It's through others that we see the human condition and ourselves. We get the boost up out of this damn ditch from others. But there's a catch. Others are also the diversion. Others are the problem and the answer to it. Our unity is the spiritual principles contained in the Twelve Steps, because that's the only thing we agree on. It does not mean that we all do the Steps in the same way.

We want to hide in our crawl spaces, heaping dirt on ourselves and making friends with the spiders. "I can do it myself. I hate you. Go away!" Yeah, whatever. Here's another plea for help from a scared human being. We have an idea! Let's go to a meeting set up some chairs. Let's go make coffee and take out the trash. Let's sit in on the business meeting and get a volunteer commitment. Commitment? I knew it would come to this! What about "one day at a time"? The commitment implies we have to show up. It now appears that "one day at a time" is a reference to my emotional sobriety. Commitment is service; commitment is a little sacrifice. Commitment is not to change others; it changes us. It's called working with others.

Tradition Two—"Trust"

So who runs the fellowship? Tradition Two tells us that it is the group conscious working together instead of a single human being. We discuss an issue until fear leaves the room and then decide or compromise, leaving room for new information to arrive. The ideal of anarchy in the beginning was that humans would voluntarily align themselves for the common good if allowed to do anything they wanted. Well, the human condition precludes this ideal from becoming reality in ordinary human affairs, but for the fellowship, we can have a kind of benign anarchy where we choose to help and cooperate with others because of our own desire to be free. We can choose to volunteer, to sacrifice time and energy, and to carry the message of freedom that the Twelve Steps promise. We can choose to trust those who do the work of the fellowship at our request.

Tradition Three—"Tolerance"

Everybody is welcome, period. There are no rules; there are no laws. It's not our job to stand at the door and demand to see your qualifications. It's our job to welcome everyone. If you don't belong, if you don't need or want us, you will not stay. We can help you find out where you need to be. You wouldn't have showed up if there were no trouble in your life. Spirituality has no sides on it. It's not in a box. If someone tells you that you can't get to the top of the mountain on a donkey named Bob, they are wrong. We all have different views and opinions on everything, but our similarities far outweigh our differences. Fear is the true basis of intolerance, so we can't be judge and jury of our own desperate brother or sister. There is one caveat, however. This is not for people who need it, and it's not for people who want it; it's for people who do it. So we welcome anyone who decides that they have a problem and help them decide where he or she ought to be.

Dig Deep in One Place

Tradition Four—"Autonomy"

We cannot believe that we survived playing with most every brand of fire. When we finally emerged out of the minefield unharmed, there before us stood the harvest of self-will and anarchy—responsibility. Instead we are autonomous, which comes from the Greek *autos* (self) and *nomos* (law). Here's the diversion again; everyone has perfect freedom to live his or her life in any way they wish. The first right in recovery is the right to be wrong. If we have the right to be wrong, then so does everyone else. Being unimpaired is a definite plus in seeing where we are wrong. Staying in contact with others is the best way. Seeing what's wrong with others is easy, but what's wrong with ourselves is invisible. Autonomy does not mean anything goes. It means keeping an eye out for harmony. This is a vital skill and takes practice. The rights of one person or group do not supersede the rights of another. Freedom and responsibility go hand in hand. The more freedom we take for ourselves, the more responsibility we have. To keep this freedom and independence, we must give them to everyone around us.

Tradition Five—"Primary Purpose"

We could not possibly help you until we got pulled from the quicksand and started to take care of ourselves. Because we have the experience of the fear and what it took to leave it behind, we have the unique ability to help. This ability does not depend on learning, eloquence, or any special skills or equipment. The experience of doing the Steps is the only requirement. We cannot give away something we don't have. Telling our personal stories pierces the wall of delusion and plants the seed of hope in another human being. From that seed, a mighty recovery can grow. But we don't snatch you from a barstool and say you don't have to suffer anymore. We don't scoop you out of the gutter and jam this down your throat. We're just asked to be prepared when you reach out for help. We are learning to act with kindness, to be nonjudgmental, and to listen. We're asked to be the example for those who don't know there is a way out. If we don't do this, our lives and sanity are in danger. Even knowing this, sex, security, and society

113

show up again. How easily diverted are we by money, food, and being a big shot? It doesn't matter how compelling all that is; it only brought us ruin. For some reason, the instincts for sex, security, and society proliferate much easier than love, light, and joy.

Tradition Six—"Humility"

We have a deep-seated conviction that the Spiritual Principles can never be tied to anything else. They are freely available to all. They are not the property of any religion, politics, organization, or institution. All spirituality is plagiarism. These ideas have been around ever since man harnessed fire. The only thing original is stupidity. "You did what? Twice?" Don't tie this to anything else. That is the fatal flaw. That would be to sin, and to sin means to miss the point. Concerning spirituality, cooperate with everyone and affiliate with no one.

Tradition Seven—"Self-Support"

When we take care of our own financial needs, we are free to run our lives exactly as we wish. We cannot be influenced by anyone threatening to withdraw resources. Self-support means more than just money. It means participating in our meetings and in our community. It means what are we doing to support our recovery from the human condition? With our enthusiasm, we invite others to participate. By contributing our experience, we bring strength and hope to others. Our experience shows two perils about money—having too much and being beholden for it. Purse strings can become the ropes that hang us. When we give, we open the gates on the river of abundance. The only thing holding the river back is ourselves. It's like holding up a sheet of plywood in the Mississippi River. No wonder we're exhausted. Put the plywood down, and climb on board. Going with the flow and contributing connect us spiritually.

Tradition Eight—"Altruism"

We are all equals sharing our experience and offering mutual support to each other. This is where we distinguish Twelfth Step work from all other work. We freely give the gift that was given to us. In one-on-one in recovery, this cannot be bought or sold; it can only be shared. Anything that diverts this process kills it. This can be the fatal flaw in sponsorship. We don't accept so much as a bottle of water for our one-on-one efforts. Every one of us holds some of the knowledge we all need. We all must participate. Getting this information out, however, does have expenses. Even dedicated volunteers cannot do this full time without pay. The work it takes to make this work possible needs reasonable wages. We pay the going rate. To receive, we have to give, and to truly give, we must know how to receive. Complete the circle. Let it come, and let it go.

Tradition Nine—"Service"

The only way to freedom is to connect. We must find a way to be the gift. The fellowship is a place to give. We can always have a job in recovery. We never knew what responsibility really meant. Show up no matter what, and bring the Spiritual Principles. This isn't about what anyone else is doing; it's about what we are doing. That doesn't mean we don't take advice or suggestions from more experienced people, but by understanding responsibility, we don't need orders from anyone. There are many leaders in a fellowship of recovery but no bosses. Since we are now able to pay attention, now we can decide what's working and what's not. If it isn't working, it can be changed. Everyone in our sphere has a voice and a vote. We learn we must stop pushing the danger button to lend undue importance to what we say. We must stop viewing with alarm. Our need to control to be safe can be put aside. There doesn't need to be a system laden with rules. That would just scare away the very people we need to help. We can trust in the Spiritual Principles to guide us.

Tradition Ten—"No Opinion (Shut Up)"

The arguments in our lives disappear at the same rate as our opinions. Most of the opinions we had weren't even our own. Someone else gave them to us: our parents, our peers, the coach, the TV, or someone we were trying to impress. Opinions are just another diversion that severely restricts our ability to help. The spiritual disease of fear affects many people in many different ways, but they all belong. We are inclusive, never exclusive. Without opinion there is no conflict, and the focus can be on recovery. There should be no outside issues. Our job as a mentor is to make another mentor, not to create a following or a congregation. Our job is not to discuss world affairs but to help us and others to gain a new perspective on our own inner reactions, the human condition, and the spiritual malady of fear and find solutions. The view from up Twelve Steps keeps getting better and better. We have now entered the bottom of a funnel and can begin to see the infinite. It will keep expanding if we will just keep going, getting simpler and simpler. What an extraordinary place to be.

Tradition Eleven—"Anonymity"

Anonymity is the public relations policy of all Twelve-Step fellowships. It's based on attraction rather than promotion, giving guidelines for use in making the public aware of these programs while maintaining personal anonymity. Our eagerness to share the Steps must be tempered with the knowledge that those who need them don't necessarily want or aren't willing to do them. Our anonymity and equality keep us humble enough to know that no individual speaks for any Twelve-Step program as a whole. This is something rare in this world: groups that wish to publicize their principles and work but not its individual members.

Personal anonymity ensures that the Twelve Steps will not be associated with any one person and demonstrates to potential members that these programs are serious about protecting anonymity. Lack of anonymity could discourage well-known people from seeking the help that's offered. There are few safe places where the famous can go to be themselves. The intent of anonymity is to keep members anonymous, not the Twelve Steps. No one is required or expected to reveal their membership in a public forum. We are responsible for informing the media of our anonymity traditions. We are ambassadors in our everyday life when we live the spiritual principles. That invites others to want to participate. Recovery groups can't be secret societies, but it's plain they can't be a vaudeville circus either. It took a while to find a safe path between these extremes.

Without exception, identification with any specific Twelve-Step group at the level of the media violates the spirit of Tradition Eleven. To speak generally about the Twelve Steps and recovery is the personal choice we have made in writing this book.

Tradition Twelve—"Sacrifice"

Anonymity is more than a denial of self-seeking; it's a constant and practical reminder of what humility is. The spiritual substance of humility is sacrifice and is embodied in anonymity. We never before realized the power anonymity provides. Anonymity embodies each Step, Tradition, and Concept by stating that what we learn in recovery is far more important than any single member. Twelve-Step groups cannot let self-appointed members present themselves as messiahs representing their group before the whole public. Without exception, principles need to come before personalities at the level of press, radio, TV, film, and the electronic media, and principles must come before our own personalities at the personal level. (see Tradition Eleven) We are anonymous at the public level, but we are not anonymous to each other. Among the spiritual concepts in anonymity are the safety and respect for our fellow members, acceptance of each other, and a desire to live by the Spiritual principles rather than reacting to the personalities around me. The Principles need to come before our personalities. Performing the service becomes the principle; the personality performing the service becomes unimportant.

CHAPTER TWELVE

Twelve Concepts of World Service

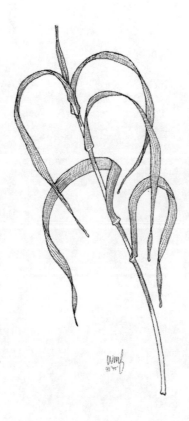

"It's not a problem, it's an opportunity"
—Bill

The Twelve Concepts
of World Service

"The Twelve Concepts of Service are a statement of our spiritual corporate purpose. They are a set of principles that guide our business relationships, they teach us how Twelfth Step work can be done on a large scale and they show us how we can apply the spiritual principles to our working relationships in our service structure."

—paraphrased from *Paths to Recovery, Alanon's Steps, Traditions and Concepts,*[4]

Interaction

1. The ultimate responsibility and authority for Fellowship world services should always reside in the collective conscience of our whole Fellowship.
2. The Service Conference of the Fellowship has become, for nearly every practical purpose, the active voice and effective conscience of our whole society in its world affairs.
3. The "Right of Decision" makes effective leadership possible.
4. The "Right of Participation" is the key to harmony.
5. The "Rights of Appeal and Petition" protect minorities and assure that they be heard and that personal grievances receive careful consideration.
6. The Conference acknowledges the primary administrative responsibility of the Trustees.

---

[4]   *Paths to Recovery, Al-anon's Steps, Traditions and Concepts*, (Virginia Beach, VA, Al-Anon Family Group Headquarters, Inc, 1997) Page 247

7. The Trustees have legal rights while the rights of the Conference are traditional.
8. The Board of Trustees delegates full authority for the routine management of the Fellowship Headquarters to its executive committees.
9. Good personal leadership at all service levels is a necessity. In the field of world service the Board of Trustees assumes the primary leadership.
10. Service responsibility is balanced by carefully defined service authority and double-headed management is avoided.
11. The World Service office is composed of standing committees, executives and staff members.
12. The spiritual foundation for the Fellowship is contained in the Warranties of Concept Twelve. The Conference shall observe the spirit of Fellowship tradition, taking care that:
    a. It never becomes the seat of perilous wealth or power;
    b. That sufficient operating fund and reserve be its prudent financial principle;
    c. That it place none of its members in position of unqualified authority over others;
    d. That it reach all important decisions by discussion, vote, and, whenever possible, by substantial unanimity;
    e. That its actions never be personally punitive nor an incitement to public controversy;
    f. That it never perform acts of government, and that, like the Fellowship it serves, it will always remain democratic in thought and action.

The Twelve Concepts are adapted and reprinted with permission of Alcoholics Anonymous World Services, Inc. Permission to reprint and adapt the Twelve Concepts of Alcoholics Anonymous does not mean that A.A. is affiliated with this program. A.A. is a program of recovery from alcoholism. Use of the Concepts in connection with programs and activities which are patterned after A.A. but which address other problems does not imply otherwise.

Dig Deep in One Place

Introduction to the Concepts

We think we're about to be issued some wings to fly above the human condition. There are some things we should have learned in kindergarten, like how to apply the spiritual principles to all our relationships; we must participate to expand our recovery. We need practical, healthy ways to arrive at decisions that involve others. Everyone has different ideas about solutions to our common problems: sharing ideas, exploring alternatives, seeking spiritual guidance, and using the newly found solutions to reach decisions we can all live with. To drop all this into gear, we have to know that the ultimate responsibility and authority for our recovery lies with us. This is the greatest gift we have ever gotten.

Our box of troubles was handed back to us but this time with a way to deal with anything that enters our lives. Trying this out using the spiritual principles as a guide on every level of our lives was awkward at first, but connecting with you is the only way it works. We have never been direct and clear about anything. Now, be clear about responsibility and authority. Be direct about policies and procedures, and act on decisions once they are made. By participating we can become informed. We can listen and add our voices and vote to any matter being considered. If we have a problem, it's our responsibility to explain. We take responsibility for the job we can do and let others assume responsibility for theirs. As a matter of fact, delegating responsibility for your life in recovery to you is the only way to help. It's an awesome gift. We set the example by encouraging everyone with love and enthusiasm. We need to give up insisting that our way is the only way a task can be done. When we do our job and let you do yours, nobody becomes overly burdened or responsible. There is no need to go to the top for every problem that occurs. Seeing what we can bring sets the principle of giving back in motion and makes any situation a gift.

Concept One—"Responsibility"

Spiritual Principles guide us at every level of our recovery. It starts with the Steps, moves through the Traditions, and continues all the way through the Concepts. Concept One poses the question: "Who is responsible for the fellowship?" The answer, as seen in Concept Two is, "We, the members of the fellowship, are responsible." We didn't like it when we discovered that we were responsible for our responses to fear. You scared us, so it must be your fault. Any situation that scared us made it the situation's fault. Today with the help of the Twelve Steps, we have a choice. We are responsible for where we are, we are responsible for where we want to be, and we have to show up to participate in our lives. The string of our lives is in our hands, and we can place it where we choose. Since we are new at this, it requires some practice. This becomes a trying-it-out process. In the beginning, we did not know what responsibility meant. Today we know that responsibility is the greatest gift that recovery from the spiritual disease of fear has to offer. It is the ability to respond. To those of us who have always just reacted, this is 180° from the habit of our lives. It means we have to pay attention; we have to persist. The only way we know how to do this is to help someone else to discover a solution.

No organization can survive without clear definitions of responsibility and authority to decide policies and procedures and to act on decisions once they are made. We are responsible for being informed with a working knowledge of the Steps, Traditions, and Concepts. Now we can participate by listening to others and adding our voices and votes to the matter being considered. We contribute our experience because it brings strength and hope. Many times we can also contribute our time, effort, and money. If we have a problem or concern, it is our responsibility to explain our viewpoint to the group.

Concept One shows us where our responsibility lies. We can't expect others to do for us what we can do for ourselves, nor do we assume responsibility for them.

Concept Two—"Delegation"

Delegation is the answer to the dilemma of how to discharge our obligation to the fellowship. Since we all cannot actually be a part of a conference, delegation begins at the group level and permeates the service structure.

On a personal level, delegation is the most powerful thing we can do for another human being. The Twelve Steps delegated responsibility to us for our lives, so we delegate to you responsibility for your life. We do this by acknowledging their presence. By picking up the tab for someone else, we are denying him or her access to a spiritual life. Until the consequences of our behavior (good or bad) became a working part of our lives, we were trapped in a downward spiral. Delegating to you the responsibility for your life and showing you how to take that responsibility is the greatest gift you can be given. We set the example by being responsible ourselves, by volunteering service to the fellowship and following through with what we say and believe. The principle of giving back what we have been given is service come to life. We rotate our positions in service so no one volunteer or worker becomes overly burdened or responsible. Once a job or function has been delegated, let that person do the job. There is no need to go to the top for every problem that occurs. We need to give up insisting that our way is the only a task can be done. We cannot do everything, nor do we want to. We are meant to be interdependent.

Concept Three—"Decision"

Remember your first right in recovery was the right to be wrong. The next three rights are the right of decision, the right of participation, and the right of appeal and petition. Without the right of decision, no leadership is possible. Without the freedom to decide how to proceed, nothing could be done. Everything would have to be checked with everyone else, no matter how trivial. I am now capable of deciding which matters to ask for help on and which to dispose of myself. What a great way to grow and learn. We trust our leaders to make right decisions and change their opinions and vote if need be. When we grant them the right of decision, our faith is in the Spiritual Principles and we trust in their integrity. When the task is delegated, some guidelines must be set, but the details are decided by the person doing the task.

Trust and confidence in them supports their competence and personal dignity. We learn how to be willing employees and effective employers. In our own life the right of decision means we have the right to proceed in the best way we know how and ask for help when it is needed.

Concept Four—"Participation"

If I decide to sit in a saloon, I will participate in that decision. I will participate in any decision I make. It's a spiritual law. Participation is the key to harmony. Belonging is a deep spiritual need. The harmony created by our active, willing participation encourages others to participate. Because of our intimate familiarity, experience, and knowledge of all these principles, we can help troubleshoot plans or give valuable, practical insights into anything being discussed! We respect each other as we ourselves want to be respected—as equals and partners on a spiritual journey. Acting as caring and understanding adults, we invite others to do the same and the likelihood of them being responsible, willing participants increases. There are two sides to participation: giving of ourselves and including others. When all of us have a chance to participate, there is less opposition and alienation. We were spiritually nourished when we were encouraged to participate, but we were never expected to carry the whole load.

Concept Five—"Appeal and Petition"

The rights of appeal and petition protect minorities and ensure that they are heard. Individual freedom and belonging are both of enormous importance to us, and we never take these rights away from anyone. We listen with consideration to everyone and encourage those with differing opinions to state their views. Hearing, understanding, evaluating, and incorporating these opinions and views help us avoid mistakes. It keeps us focused and validates the worth and dignity of everyone. It keeps us from being angry, hasty, misinformed, and rigid. Everyone has not only the right but also the duty to speak out. It takes courage to speak if you are the minority, but with permission and even obligation without fear of reprisal, that courage will be strengthened. Listening to everyone may bring to mind a solution that hadn't been thought of before. This could be better than a compromise. Respectfully listening and carefully considering everyone's suggestions ensures that each of us will always be a valued participant. It is important and necessary that everyone feels included.

Petition permits anyone with a personal grievance to be heard without fear of prejudice or reprisal. The mere existence of the right of petition, even if it's not often used, restrains the use of authority. So, if you decide to go to that saloon and participate in that decision, you can appeal. "Can I make a different choice?" "Yes! Keep coming back!"

Concept Six—"Guidance"

Who does what and why reminds us to acknowledge where the primary responsibility lies, to grant others enough freedom to do a job and provide workable guidelines that keep visions and goals clearly in mind. We treat others as we would like to be treated without nitpicking or over managing. Responsibility without power is both ineffective and unhealthy, while power without responsibility is an invitation to dominance. Efficient and effective business operations help us to achieve our primary purpose—presenting the Spiritual Principles.

Concept Seven—"Accountability"

A board of directors/trustees would have legal rights, while volunteer rights are traditional. The board is entrusted with the guardianship of legal status, rights, and finances. We are guided by the group conscience of the entire fellowship. The reason it works is that nobody has a vested interest; we are all volunteers. Our traditional rights are contained in the Steps, Traditions, and Concepts of the fellowship. The authority of a board of trustees is practical because it ensures our decisions are consistent with the laws that govern us and the well being of our fellowship as a whole. Interpreting of the laws as they pertain to our fellowship is part of the board's job, and the members of the board are selected at least in part for their expertise in these areas. The fellowship and board are each important, and neither becomes a rubber stamp for the other. When the fellowship acknowledges the rights, duties, and responsibilities of the board, a respectful and harmonious working relationship can be maintained. Our spiritual democracy is maintained by respect for the fellowship's traditional authority, which is backed by the power of the membership.

Concept Eight—"Authority"

The board delegates authority for operations to the people who are there and doing the job. The board possesses long-range vision for our future, but everyday management and details are in the hands of those who are doing it. It's striving to keep a balance between our volunteer fellowship and our need to provide dependable service.

We need both leaders and managers, the leaders to hear us and provide the big vision and the managers to take the steps that make accomplishing that vision possible. It takes all of us. Like snowflakes, all of us are needed to cover the ground.

Concept Nine—"Leadership"

Good personal leadership at all service levels is a necessity. But who are the leaders? Each and every person who has the courage to step forward has the potential to become a leader. Knowing the service structure of the fellowship and rotating through it provides many opportunities to develop leaders. Rotating service ensures that no one person gains control and that the joys of service can be shared by many. Leadership should offer choices and perhaps emphasize aspects, but leave it up to our fellowship to make the decisions. A detached, clearheaded ability to respond with courage and creativity is a quiet strength we seek in our leaders and in ourselves.

Good personal leadership at all service levels means welcoming anyone new into our fellowship. One interesting side effect of this entire process, this ability to see ourselves so clearly, is that we can see everyone else with equal clarity. Recovery is not necessarily the land of the well. Dealing with all these erratic individuals will often take everything you have. Bad behavior and anger are fear announced and are often calls for help. Patience and careful listening are essential. Sometimes what's said may have some truth. Other times it may be just nonsense, but it all needs a hearing. In all cases we must take our own inventory and continue to practice the Spiritual Principles.

Concept Ten—"Balance of Power"

In volunteer service, responsibility should be balanced by carefully defined service authority. This authority ensures that no two people or groups will be equally responsible for the outcome of any project. In all areas of our lives, we need to be clear about what our responsibilities are. If we are given large responsibilities and no authority, leadership is impossible. Without the necessary authority to complete a task, it is natural to assume less and less responsibility or pass the buck. When delegated authority is working well, it is best to leave it alone. And don't forget there are many ways to do a job. Watch, listen, and learn.

Concept Eleven—"Cooperation"

In service many committees can be formed, composed of executives and staff members. Anyone doing service can consider themselves a member of one or more of these committees. The clear description of what these committees are and the status of the people involved, who's paid, and what their jobs are. Competent and sustained executive direction must be headed up by one person. Paid workers should receive comparable wages for service or abilities in the business world. Cheap help feels insecure and will be inefficient. It is neither good spirituality nor good business. Rotation and equal pay assures security and continuity of the job. Everyone participates fully, paid workers and volunteers.

Concept Twelve—"Prudence"

Prudence now appears as a middle ground between fear on one side and recklessness on the other. What does this look like, and what does it promise?

Here are the things we promise we won't do, and here are the things we promise we will do. Power and wealth are perilous and require persistent scrutiny. The preceding discussion embraces and explains how to keep it in check. At the same time, it is evident that we need sufficient operating funds, reminding us to take care of ourselves financially without excessive spending or stockpiling. We will not put absolute authority in the hands of one individual. We will reach all decisions by substantial unanimity. This reinforces participation and the opinion of the minority. There will be no punitive action. We willingly follow the unenforceable. Here's what's unenforceable again: acceptance, open mindedness, willingness, honesty, love, forgiveness, harmony, truth, faith, hope, light, and joy. We don't make rules and punish those who break them. We do not need to defend ourselves against criticism. This is not a doctrine that needs to be maintained. There is no prestige to defend, no power, pride, or property worth fighting over. If our critics are justified, we thank them and take our own inventory. Peace is our goal, and the best defense is simply setting a good example. This means always being democratic in thought and action. "In thought" means keeping an open mind and granting the same dignity to others' ideas as we do our own. "In action" means to remember the greatest good, prudent financial management, keeping principles before personalities, and welcoming all those who wish to belong. We act with firmness and kindness and without anger, haste, recklessness, or control.

What a statement of corporate policy! Practice these principles in all our affairs, principles before personalities, and democratic in thought and action. With this as our starting gate, we are truly blessed to have such a simple recipe for action to take.

It is now possible to change the Universe one person at a time. If we want to get there, all we have to do is go! What we need will be provided.

CHAPTER THIRTEEN

Love, Light, and Joy—Recovery and Art

"Do it or don't, but the whining is over."
—Bill

"May we live, love, and give with a grateful heart."
—Sandy

What Is Recovery?

What do we mean by recovered? Recovered from what? We couldn't imagine a day without fear. We believe that all humans are afflicted with the spiritual malady of fear to one extent or another. For humans, the primal fears are that we may freeze, starve, or be eaten. Today, though these events are remote possibilities, we still have unreasonable fear, but we call it stress, anxiety, panic attacks, depression, anger, or resentment. There is no saber-toothed tiger around the corner, yet these fears persist with new names.

Human beings are incredible. We could and did create all sorts of behaviors to deal with these fears. We tried to control those around us by domination or depending on them too much. We attempted to control our world with food, drugs, alcohol, material things, relationships, and sex. We became obsessed with the idea that these fears would subside if we just practiced these self-destructive behaviors hard enough or managed our circumstances just a little better.

Our own willingness to perform the actions called for in the thirty-six Spiritual Principles (Steps, Traditions, and Concepts) brought us to the starting gate where we could begin to practice a spiritual life. What is a spiritual life? It's helpfulness to others, seeing ourselves in others without fear, to be aware of our true motives and actions, to see "who and what we really are followed by a sincere attempt to become what we could be."

Before we were introduced to the thirty-six Spiritual Principles, we had no choice. We could do nothing but react to the circumstances and situations in our lives. Recovery from fear started with a clear look at ourselves.

Bill and Sandy Fifield

Forgiveness

It wasn't as if we had never practiced any principles in our lives. We were both from good families who taught us right from wrong and the basics of human relationships—honesty, love, and forgiveness—but the idea of actually practicing these ideals didn't seem real. We had no idea how to deliberately do them or why. Sometimes it just happened and it worked. The results were incredible.

A case in point: Like a pall over our lives was the trouble with our neighbors. We had moved to the mountains southwest of Denver looking for a place to establish our art studio. We found the perfect spot with a large fifty-by-fifty-foot corrugated steel building. It had been a horse barn but would be perfect for creating custom furniture and stained glass. The property was ten acres and had two small houses as well. It was perfection. We worked hard to renovate the horse barn and houses. We had no close neighbors for five years.

It started innocently enough—a family from Denver bought a small sliver of land between us and the highway. We both used the same access road, which is the paved portion of the old highway. We were not pleased at the thought of neighbors so close, but in an attempt to be neighborly, we helped by providing water and electricity in the beginning. We lent tools and digging equipment as well to facilitate building a foundation. Next they moved an old brick house all the way up from Denver. This blocked the access road for three days.

Now requests for help became demands at 6:00 a.m. several times a week. Needless to say, we did not respond well. All of a sudden we had a mortal enemy. We were baffled by the fact that relations just kept getting worse and worse. There always seemed to be another piece of bad news created by these people. We began to spend hours and hours talking about what they did and our resentments against them. It became our sole subject of conversation, ad nauseam.

They built a chain-link fence, then a concrete wall down the center of our access road and then sued us over the road access. We were forced at great expense to get rezoned to have our studio/workshop. They stole our Scottie dog, Winston, and then our new puppy, Carlyle. We never recovered Winston but with the help of a wonderful county sheriff were able to retrieve the Carlyle from them. They recruited our neighbor to the east in on the fun. This was the old cowboy they had purchased their land from. He sued us over the property line to the east, moving it about a thousand feet in from the original line, and had his hired hand patrol the property line armed to the teeth with guns and knives. They made accusations to the sheriff's department about anything they could think of, from burying trash on their property at midnight (naked) to allowing our dog to chase elk. It seemed never ending. We hated them. We were scared to death. It was costing a fortune, and everything we had worked for was being threatened.

We thought we had tried everything to deal with this ongoing onslaught of negativity: defiance, defense, resistance, resentment, and retaliation. We retained a lawyer and fought back in court, but we seemed to be powerless. Even the county government seemed to be on their side.

In the midst of all this, we jokingly said to each other, "Why don't we kill them with kindness?" (At the time we probably deep down wanted this to actually happen.) We had no idea where the idea came from, but it worked. We would smile and wave while they just stood there with arms crossed, glaring at us. At that point, the tide turned. We actually won the lawsuit over the access. The wall and fence stayed, and even though our access was only one lane wide, some trees grew up the middle, and it even looks sort of pretty today. We were able to rezone to accommodate our art studio. They stopped glaring at us and even tentatively tried to respond in kind. They eventually moved back to Denver and began renting the property to people who knew nothing about the conflict. The old cowboy eventually dropped his lawsuit without taking any of our land. We had ceased to resent. We had withdrawn from the contest. We had changed our thinking—how? By changing our actions. We stopped reacting in fear and started to take the simple actions of smiling and waving instead.

We didn't realize just how powerful this was at the time. It wasn't until years later that we discovered there was a recipe to come to forgiveness. Forgiveness is not to condone or excuse bad behavior. Forgiveness is to cease to resent. Resentment is poison. We drink the poison of resentment and wait for the other person to die. Without forgiveness, we are the ones who die—sometimes physically, always spiritually.

After we were introduced to the Steps, we began to learn more about this powerful principle of forgiveness. On looking back at our behavior at the time, it becomes clear that even if forgiveness is motivated by selfish desires, it works to begin to relieve the bitterness and hatred that come from fear and therefore make any situation more peaceful.

Tangible Results

During the summer of 1998 to facilitate the remodel of our house, we moved all our furniture up to our studio to do some fancy camping for three months while we gutted and replaced everything in the house, but there were no closets. It was, after all, a wood, welding, and glass workshop. We had an old tall kitchen cabinet left over from some project that Sandy wanted converted into a closet to store our clothes. Reverting back into old behavior, instead of directly asking for help, she attempted to manipulate Bill into having the idea himself. This immediately precipitated old behavior in Bill that took the form of anger or you might say rage. Bill stormed out of the room ranting about how he didn't work on old pieces of shit made of toxic waste held together with staples and camel piss . . . Suddenly, as if hearing himself for the first time, he stopped, turned around, re-entered the room, and said, "Let me rephrase that. I would be happy to fix this cupboard. What would you like to have done?" Now the ball was back in Sandy's court. Past behavior would have demanded a retort sounding something like this: "It's too late, big boy, you're going to pay for this one!" but when she opened her mouth, out came a direct request for the closet she needed. So instead of a week of strained relations and fighting, we had an awesome day of laughter and partnership and working together instead of pouting and silent scorn. How amazing to have a real choice and actually use it. It was the tangible result of practicing Spiritual Principles.

Reunion—Sandy's Son

In February 1965 I gave my infant son up for adoption. Although there was some wishful thinking over the years, I had not regretted this decision because I knew that the selfish and self-centered behavior that marked those years would not have been a peaceful family life for any child.

In 1996 he would be thirty-one years old. In that same year, I had four years of recovery and felt confident that I could handle an attempt to contact him. Colorado is an open adoption state, so I was able to petition the court for an intermediary who would actually make contact. I agreed that if he wanted nothing to do with me, I would drop the matter. I believe that every child has a right to know who his birth mother is for many reasons—medical, emotional, and psychological. I hoped that he would want to meet me.

The first thing I found out was that his name was Michael and that he had grown up in Denver. The intermediary found him in Atlanta, where he was in training to be a pilot. She contacted him with the news that I wanted to connect. At first he refused, saying that he didn't need to know, that it didn't matter, and that he didn't want to hurt his adoptive mother. He did agree, however, to receive a letter from me.

This was my chance to make my amend to him. I wrote a short letter of introduction, admitted my mistakes, and told him that if he wished, I was definitely open to meeting him and honestly answering any questions he might have. We exchanged photos. He looked so much like my father, and he wanted to be a pilot. This started a yearlong correspondence culminating in Michael coming to my house to meet Bill, my mother, and me. There was no drama, and he actually spent the night with us. There were many questions asked and answered on both sides over that incredible weekend. We have since become great friends, and Michael has become a part of our family in every way possible.

Shit Truck or Fertilizer Wagon?

It was a typical trip to Denver to run some errands and pick up supplies for a project we had in the studio, but nothing seemed to go easily. Parking spaces evaporated before our eyes, and there were bad drivers and rude clerks. Circumstances became more and more annoying, and Sandy was becoming more and more irritable and frustrated. Bill said, "Let's use the Spiritual Principles of the program to deal with this onslaught of negativity!" Sandy's response to this was: "I'm not in the mood. I'm irritated, and I'm certain that it won't work here anyway." Bill asked sweetly, "Have you prayed about it?" Sandy quickly retorted, "Of course I have, damn it, and I don't want to hear about it again!" And so it went. The more irritated Sandy got, the more spiritual Bill got. The symptoms of the obsession were back, and it seemed to be getting worse. After a full day, it was finally time to start home. Sandy could hardly wait to get home and be out of the car that had become way too small for the both of them.

We were delighted to finally turn onto our road from the highway but startled to see the truck that had turned in just before us continue up our driveway. As the road narrowed to one lane, the truck stopped, and the driver got out and walked through a gate to a storage building on our neighbors' property. Sandy tooted the horn, but the gentleman completely ignored her and continued to disappear within the building. "How dare he do this to *me?*" Sandy exclaimed. "What's the matter with that guy?" She really honked the horn this time. "Wait a minute," said Bill. "This might be the perfect time for us to practice the Spiritual Principles. How about acceptance and a little forgiveness?" But Sandy was way too far into her anger and couldn't see anything else. Sandy honked the horn again and still no one came out to move the truck and unblock the driveway, but we did catch a glimpse of the fellow peeking around the corner. It's obvious that he was not coming out. We were stuck! Bill suggested turning around and taking the back road into our property. "The guy is scared to death, there are no windows in that building so he can't see us, and he could be stuck in there for hours. Let it go." Sandy said, "No! It's too late and too far! Absolutely not. I won't do it!" Bill replied, "I know, but let's see what happens if we do." Sandy finally surrendered and said, "Okay, let's do it."

We turned around, and within five minutes, we were home. Something had changed. The fact that she could not change the situation dawned on Sandy. She realized that the man in the truck really was scared, at least as much or maybe more than she was. He couldn't possibly have known our history with the owners of the property because he was just renting the storage building. Suddenly Sandy was excited at the way the Spiritual Principles had worked in spite of her extreme resistance. As she surrendered to these very simple ideas, our life was becoming more and more peaceful. Sandy could finally laugh at the way she had acted all day. We blessed the man stuck in the building, and we actually hoped that he didn't spend the whole afternoon hiding from us.

Reconnection—Bill's Family

Communication with my folks was spotty at best after I escaped from Minnesota and got even worse as I became more of a prisoner of my obsession. My amends to my parents started as an occasional phone call for a while and ended up as a call every Sunday morning at 9:00 a.m. My dad had lots of questions about the Twelve Steps, and they became the basis of our conversations. My mom was just thrilled that I was back in the land of the living and bragged to everyone who would listen that I had invented the Twelve Steps. In her mind I was in line for sainthood. On the other hand, Dad was his old suspicious and cynical self. After fifteen years of calls, with me telling him that I loved him at the end of our talks, he one day said that he loved me back. I started to cry. It was wonderful. Four months later, he died suddenly. It was sad, and I miss him very much, but there was no hair-tearing grief. We were clean; we had said everything that needed to be said. When I got the news, the thing that popped into my head was overwhelming gratitude for all the gifts he had given me. He taught me how to build a cardboard box for anything you could think of, a skill I use at least every Christmas season. He taught me to stand before a blank piece of paper with no fear of creation and joy in my heart. Thank you, Dad. God bless you.

The Portals of Creation—Sandy

My parents were both creative and artistic. My father illustrated his letters with small, funny, cartoon drawings, but my mother had a talent that was diverted by marriage and motherhood. Like many young women, she was fascinated by fashion illustration, at which she was very good. She sometimes painted in watercolor and sculpted in clay when the opportunity presented itself. I remember a clay portrait of my sister that really captured her spirit. I believe my parents were supportive of my early efforts at drawing, painting, and crafts.

Where then did I pick up the belief that I was not good at art, that I couldn't draw a straight line? The Twelve Steps helped me to uncover the source of that belief.

Ask a group of first graders, "Who can sing, dance, draw, and paint?" Way more than half will enthusiastically raise their hands, jump up and down, and cry, "Me, me! I can, I can!" Ask a similar group of sixth graders the same question and the response is amazingly different; maybe only two or three will raise their hands. What has happened? The lie has wormed its way into the minds and hearts of these young people. It is only one manifestation of the lie that I am not good enough and I will never be good enough.

I remember the moment when the lie was given to me in regards to my artistic talent. I was around ten years old, having a great time working on an assignment for my school art class. We were to carve and sand a piece of wood into an abstract shape. It was great fun to work off each other's ideas when the teacher told me that obviously I would never be an artist because my creation was similar to my friend's work. I was devastated. I started to cry and refused to finish the project at all. I believed this man's narrow view of what art and creativity are and began to gather evidence to support my supposed failure at art.

I have come to believe that he was wrong, that there is really is nothing new under the sun, that creativity is the unique interests, techniques, and journeys that reside within each individual, that true creativity lies in the combination of these ideas and interests into truly new and exciting manifestations in any field of human endeavor, and that if I want to draw a straight line, I can use a ruler. This is art, but it can also include everything that humans can possibly do to make their lives and the lives of others more serene, harmonious, beautiful, productive, or safe.

I have been creating beautiful and unique jewelry, stained glass, beveled glass, and fused glass for forty-five years in spite of my belief in the lie. My journey through the Twelve Steps has given me the ability to expose and confront this belief that tells me that I am not good enough and will never be good enough. Today my prayer is, "I stand at the portals of creation; I am willing to receive."

Is My Art Really in the Bottle?—Bill

My first commission after I got out of Harmony was to carve sixteen life-sized mountain men busts. These were to be used as shelf supports over the windows in an Evergreen man's trophy room. Since I was convinced that my art and talent had all been in bottle of booze or a bag of cocaine, I was sure that this was going to be an embarrassing failure. I put the commission off for as long as possible by taking photos of every interesting male face I could find and working and reworking one drawing to the point of shredding the paper.

Finally all my excuses were exhausted and I started carving. The first one took a month and a half. My God! It was great! It really looked like a mountain man, all grizzly and tough. I thought, *Maybe it wasn't the booze and the dope. Maybe the creativity was so strong it showed through in spite of the substances.* The next fifteen carvings took just three weeks, and I was thrilled with the results.

My willingness to do the Steps, Traditions, and Concepts forms a triangle: recovery, unity, and service. It's like a three-legged stool: very stable, but it takes all three legs. Something that is seldom discussed or understood is the circle surrounding the triangle. To me this is the intuition, the creativity. It's sitting in God's pocket. It's intuitively knowing how to handle situations that used to baffle me. It's learning to trust my creative process.

The blank piece of paper of creativity no longer scares me. My experience has shown that if I will go, what I need will come. Like

Indiana Jones stepping off into the abyss, he did not fall; a bridge appeared. I did not fall, I flew. Today I don't know what will come, but it has *never* been bad. The wood talks to me today. I start with a commission or an idea and then let the universe direct me. It's a miracle, not magic. Magic was in a bottle or a bag. The miracle requires my active, positive participation. The miracle waits for you. It's yours for the taking. Come help yourself.

CHAPTER FOURTEEN

Passing it On—The Circle of Recovery

"May your journey be sharp and narrow as a sword."
—Bill

This chapter consists of the stories of seven people we have taken through the Steps.

Rob—Despair Took a Nosedive

My sister handed me the phone as I lay stunned in a hospital bed. I had once again torn my life apart. My wife was talking about giving up on me. My one-year-old son was held hostage by my addiction.

I recognized the voice on the other end of the line as Bill said, "Hello?" That hello greets me most every day now as we continue a journey that saved my life and more.

I had heard him share at meetings. He was outrageous. He had a gravely, low voice. A giant of a man hurling truth into the room like some sweet recovery cake batter. It splattered across that dusty place, coated the walls, and dripped down into the worn couches and chairs. The people in the room were startled, cajoled, accosted. Some smiled. Others leaned back into the dusty folds of ancient stained cushions and breathed in the hope, sensed the promise, absorbed the light and the joy that would surely come if they did as this man did.

My own story is simple. Unaware of how to live my life, engulfed by fear, I was overrun. Time and again I turned to the only hope I knew, alcohol and drugs. For a while that approach brought relief and precipitous heights of joy and confidence. And then it brought despair. I hardly noticed the change or accepted the loss. I kept at it, chasing that elusive, fractious relief. Despair took a nosedive. I experienced the "incomprehensible demoralization" that so many of my kind know so well.

Here I was again. The stakes were higher. The people affected were more innocent. The story was old, sad, and tired.

On the phone I told Bill a little and his response was immediate. "Great!" he said. "That is just perfect! Now we can begin!" Begin what I could not comprehend, but this man sensed promise where I saw tragedy. I glimpsed a light.

I began to meet with him. I was scared. I felt limited and inept. He said I was teachable. He started to reveal a new way of living, free of the old lie of chemical salvation. He began to guide me into a program of recovery, give to me what to him was given. I placed him on high, so versed in this program I wanted. He asked everything of me and possessed a joy at which I clumsily leapt in wonder.

And still today he asks everything. He reminds me that I was warned. And I was. "The spiritual path is not for the faint of heart," he said. "Who would undertake such a journey? Those who had no other course but death." His voice would soften at this unerring fact. Bill does not dress up the truth. Nuance and subtlety are not in his quiver. He speaks as if his and many other lives depend on the veracity of his message. He is on fire, and there are many lives returned to men who have gathered 'round, taken action, and passed the message on.

Bill asks for my best and reminds me who I am and what's at stake. He gives me the key, the hardest task, the most fruitful endeavor. He asks me to help another, to make that the great fact of my existence. He reveals to me that my path through the universe is marked by those I've given to, not taken from.

My affection for Bill is profound, my gratitude unending. My tendency to take him for granted is ubiquitous. I build him up and tear him down. I receive his gift daily, and he is always there. I'd be worse than dead without him, and yet he is just a man. He carries a message. It is a message so pure and powerful that those not ready recoil, as it strikes deep into their fear, seeking to expose it.

Those ready rejoice and marvel at the simple spiritual beauty before them.

Kelly—Getting Sober with Sandy

I met Sandy within a few days of coming into our local Twelve Step fellowship club. She asked easy questions that I could answer by nodding or shaking my head. I was too afraid to speak. She told me the very basics—that the program worked and I wouldn't have to drink

Dig Deep in One Place

again. She introduced me to the Twelve Steps and Twelve Traditions. She briefly explained how sponsorship worked.

I was sooooooo afraid, yet desperate to figure out how to live without a drink. A couple days after we met, I asked if she would sponsor me. She said she would be "honored." That confused me; how could anyone feel honored to spend time with me? She asked me to call her every day and read the first twenty-three pages of the *Big Book*, and we would meet on Monday nights.

Monday night she rode with me to her house, essentially across the street (but in the mountains that means about a half-mile drive). I'm not sure which is scarier, driving drunk (which I was used to) or newly sober, still shaking, with a very sober person in the car. She had such courage, faith, or both. We got to the studio, where Sandy makes stained glass and has a room just for meeting with women. It has a small table and chairs, lots of books, and various art creations. When we met, we held hands and said the Serenity prayer; then she read to me. As she read, she would stop and explain things to me. I recall from our first meeting she explained things such as all the places mood altering substances hide in my house—mouthwash, cooking spray, vanilla extract, etc.—and suggested removing them all. This was my first experience in building in "pause." If it wasn't in my house, I'd have to think about it and take deliberate action to go get it. Hopefully, a second thought would enter my head, or God would intervene before I could actually get a drink to my lips. She also told me she couldn't promise that my husband would come back or that my life would look a certain way; however, she did tell me that if I did this work, I would be happy.

I called every day. Sandy usually answered and thanked me for calling. Whenever I called with a question or problem and she was unavailable, she would call me back. The act of calling taught me that every day I was seeking the solution; it connected me with another person; and it helped me to memorize her number, in case I ever really wanted to drink and my cell phone was unavailable or didn't work. (That has helped me several times, not just for drinking but also for the return of my obsessive thinking.)

Sandy and I met once a week and went over the reading assignment she had given me. I read the assignments nearly every day because my reading comprehension and concentration were nonexistent. Even with reading it daily, it always sounded different and had deeper meaning when Sandy read it to me.

Many of the suggestions that Sandy gave me were just plain weird to me. The learning may be in taking the action, but the understanding of it always came in hindsight. She would suggest things like, "Take your dogs for a walk." This helped me stop thinking about myself and my problems. She would tell me to take God with me, literally. I went to a concert and literally opened the passenger door; invited God in; fastened the seatbelt; and closed the door. When I got to the concert, I opened the door, unbuckled the belt, let God out, and asked that he stay between me and a drink. It worked; I was able to enjoy a concert sober. What a trip. Sandy told me to look for a gift in things. Sometimes that felt like an Easter egg hunt. She would tell me to see what I could bring (and she didn't mean a pie). The suggestions seemed odd, but they worked, and I still use them.

On Step Three we did something I had not done since I went to church camp at around age thirteen. We prayed the Third Step prayer together on our knees. Praying holding hands is one thing, but together on our knees is a very different, moving experience, one that I will never forget. As I remember that night, it never ceases to re-create that intense emotional reaction of an awareness that this was a sure and significant change in my life. I reconnected with God, even though I didn't understand what that meant.

Sandy provided specific instructions for the "hard" written Steps Four and Nine. The formats were easy to follow and provided enough of a framework for me to follow, yet I was able to make them uniquely my own. She didn't tell me what to say but gave me the blueprint for how to say it. She even warned me that some have significant reactions and told me what to do about them: "call." All those daily phone calls paid off. The phone, although still quite heavy, was not quite as difficult to pick up. In Step Four my self-pity returned to the point of auditory hallucinations, in the form of my closest liquor store calling my name, luring me back. I picked up the phone and called people until I got a real person. Answering machines weren't going to cut it. The pull to drink had not been this strong in many weeks. The "tools" that Sandy was teaching me worked again.

Throughout the time we met, Sandy encouraged me to do things I didn't want to do, such as say hello to the new person that comes into a meeting; wash the coffee cups; pick up the club; participate; and the really hard one, share in the meetings. She supported as I walked through each of these, as well as when I faced each fear in other aspects of my life. She taught me how to say, "I don't know" and not feel like I was a piece of crap for not knowing. She taught me how to say, "I was wrong;" to take real responsibility for my behavior. In the process, the "I was wrong" actually translated to a thank you for showing me exactly what I needed to see. I couldn't have learned this lesson in any other way.

Most of all Sandy showed me how to give "this thing" away to any person who is desperate enough to do it. Sandy calmly demonstrated to me how to practice spiritual principles in all aspects of my life. She showed me ways to serenely refuse to participate in the chaos and drama my addiction drives me toward. Her encouragement to relentlessly pursue the practice of a spiritual life provided the courage I needed to walk through my fears.

Beyond the Twelve Steps of recovery, we went through the Traditions and Concepts of fellowship groups. I gained a clearer understanding of groups and relationships, both in and out of the program. Sandy helped instill the desire that I want to give back to the group and club that helped save my life.

The Concepts helped me understand the loose structure of fellowship groups. Although very dry and seemingly boring, Sandy explained them in a way that was personal to my recovery, as well as related to the fellowship as a whole. I want this organization to be intact and available for those who come looking for a way out of the disease of alcoholism. Being of service to the fellowship as a whole is part of that. It also teaches me how to interact with others.

I knew early on that Sandy would never ask me to do something she had not done herself. She never told me what I had to do; she explained what had worked for her and showed me how to apply the principles to my own situations. The entire process of the weekly meetings took approximately eight to nine months. In that time I was given a new life. Sandy has been, and continues to be, my example, my mentor, my sponsor, and my friend. For that I am truly grateful.

Marya—Change of Attitude

I was working with a good sponsor, and I had completed most of the Twelve Steps with her, but she was not able to continue sponsoring me. I had to find another sponsor in order to continue recovering. Lucky for me, she told me about Bill, and he was available to sponsor.

Even though my path of recovery was unusual because I was a nonalcoholic woman using A.A. literature and a male sponsor, I believe it was orchestrated by my Higher Power, and it certainly has worked very well for me.

Right away I found out that Bill was just as serious about helping me recover as I was about recovering. He spoke directly to my questions without sugarcoating anything. Needless to say, this immediately brought out my control issues. I frequently argued with him, sometimes yelling and sometimes crying. Sometimes I was so angry with him I thought about quitting. The thing is, I knew what he was saying to me was absolutely true, so I kept calling.

I was stuck in a victim mindset. Even though I had come to the realization a year before that it was useless to go on blaming others for the problems in my life, I was still having difficulty finding new ways to behave.

With Bill I learned to stop opening my mouth every time I thought I had some important point to make, because these were usually criticisms of others or some negative comment. I learned to step away from discussions that were turning into arguments that were going nowhere and just getting uglier. I learned how to stay calm during an argument and to keep the discussion on track without becoming controlling, insulting, or negative myself. I learned to be direct in my speech and that I should pay attention to the words I use, because words have power. I was dealing with un-recovered individuals, and these tools gave me the chance I needed for a happy life. I realized that it didn't matter at all what my spouse was doing, that I could have a happy life by just focusing on my own behavior and changing it with the help of my Higher Power. I became a less demanding person but also a person who stands up for herself in a healthy, positive way. Bill taught me how important it is to pull negative thoughts and fears out of my head where they are doing damage and out into the light, where they can be dealt with. He taught me to recognize when someone is "baiting me" into the negativity of fear, whether they are doing it on purpose or not, and to not take the bait. I learned to make amends to others when needed. I learned how to handle resentments by calling my sponsor or doing a Tenth Step. From being a passive-aggressive victim I took charge of my own life and behavior.

Bill has helped me to realize that my employment is my love and service to others, and even on days when life feels mundane and boring, opportunities abound for me to share my knowledge with others. His directness with me helped me to be direct with others, something that was always difficult for me to do because of my people-pleasing tendencies. He taught me to be honest but not brutally honest. He also taught me about having boundaries by showing me that he was valuing himself by not taking calls all hours of the day or night or by not sitting around waiting for someone to show up to be sponsored when they are late for our meetings. I learned my time is valuable and my personal life is valuable.

One of the best things he taught me about sponsorship is that everyone is responsible for their own recovery. If a person dropped me as their sponsor, they just weren't ready to let go of their old behaviors yet. I realized it wasn't personal and to have compassion for them and to let them know the door is always open to them to return and recover when they are ready.

He helped me not to pre-judge an event as negative because I might be surprised at how it would turn out in the long run. He helped me to think about God in a trusting way, that either God is or God isn't.

Even though we don't share the same conception of a higher power, he respected my beliefs and I learned through that to do the same with others. He really opened my heart to having compassion for others without enabling them in a way that turned around and damaged me, something I had been trying to figure out for years.

Reviewing this, you might think that everything about his sponsorship has been perfect. I'm not saying that it was, but that in itself helped me a great deal to see that I don't have to be perfect to help people. I just have to show up and be willing. And Bill has always done that for me. I feel that I could never thank him enough for his kindness in taking time out of his own life to help me with mine.

I need to make it clear that I certainly don't utilize all these wonderful recovery behaviors all the time or as well as I would like, but the point is that I have the tools now because of my work with Bill and I will always have them. It's up to me to pick them up and use them. Sometimes I amaze myself at how well I do, and sometimes I amaze myself at my failures.

I will always be grateful to my Higher Power for finding a sponsor for me like Bill. I will always be grateful to Bill for sponsoring me so well, and I often pray that I may sponsor others as well. Being a sponsor myself is a very difficult job, and I often have turned to Bill for guidance and encouragement, and he never lets me down.

Diana—Relapse

The relapse that almost killed me turned out to be the moment that I became willing to learn and practice the thirty-six spiritual principles. Miracles are funny things for me. They don't seem to show up the way I expect them to, but they keep showing up over and over now that my head is clear and my eyes can see.

The first miracle is that I am still alive. The second is that the obsession to drink is gone. The third is that I am free to enjoy my life because I have a way to solve problems that works every time, all the time, if I do it.

The last time I drank left me feeling as though my insides were on fire, hyperventilating in fear, and shaking uncontrollably. There was a bewildered friend trying to help, then stunned bystanders, and then an ambulance guy quietly asking me if alcohol had played a role

Dig Deep in One Place

in the outcome I was experiencing today. Then the emergency room staff had to strap me down on the gurney so I didn't pull out all the tubes and needles they had running out of me. Then there was a nurse shaking her head as she recited my blood alcohol level. Finally there was my angry, ashamed husband clenching his jaw and shoving his fists in his pockets.

That was the last research project. That was coming to the understanding that alcohol was a solution that did not work anymore. That was proving to myself that drinking the way I drank would kill me. That was when I truly understood that without help, I would not survive. That was the end of a four-month relapse. That was Step One. I was powerless over alcohol, and manageability clearly was not on board. I felt terror, bewilderment, frustration, and despair.

How did I get here? My parents are both golf professionals, not alcoholics, but they both have relatives who are. There is that genetic component. Sure, I smoked a lot of pot in my teenage years. It was much easier to get than alcohol. *The real deal for me is that I was an adrenalin junkie.* I am living proof that it is possible to get from Vail to Denver in under an hour because Maserati makes a hell of a ride if you're willing to push it, and I was. I lived life on the edge.

I lived out of my car for several years off and on by choice while I was a nationally ranked sport climber. I am a multiple member of the sixty-footer club. You earn that by falling over sixty feet. Nothing made me feel more alive.

I chose to marry a climber and had a child. Then came the education about what happens when two adult children have to grow up because they have a child of their own. I wouldn't wish what we did and said to each other on anyone. Yet, I am deeply grateful to my former husband for all he has taught and continues to teach me about the vagaries of the human condition—both mine and his. I really can say I wish him all the best, and I hope he finds a solution that works for him. Mine is in this program.

I did not drink alcoholically until I was forty-two years old. My son was just over a year old. I drank alone. I drank to escape. There was nothing pretty about it. It was never fun. It was only to stop the pain for a little while. The first time I sought help, I had been drinking without being able to stop on my own for about a year and a half. It started with a couple of glasses of wine in the afternoon and quickly escalated to more than half a quart of rum every day.

Sandy was my sponsor then, and she took me through the Steps, Traditions, and Concepts. It kept me sober for almost seven years, but sober is not recovered. Recovery for me now means that I have to be around like-minded people who are actively engaged in the program. It means I call my sponsor. I go to several meetings a week. I sponsor. I carry the message because now I have a clearer idea of what truly being of service is. My life has a deep, abiding purpose, and I am content with that.

Six hours after being discharged from that emergency room, I was sitting in a meeting. Two weeks later, I was sitting across a table from Sandy beginning the steps again. Clearing away the wreckage took time. There were amends to make and friends to reconnect with. There was a twelve-year marriage that couldn't grow to embrace this change and had to be let go. There was the move to a new home and the army of friends who helped me do it.

I don't know exactly when I stopped thinking that everything was going to go wrong and instead started noticing how most things resolved quite well if I just kept doing this work to the best of my ability, but it started around Step Four and just kept growing and growing. Today I am the single, self-employed mother of a ten-year-old child. I do not regret having a child, being a mother, or my alcoholism. I understand now that sometimes life has to fall completely apart to come together. Sandy is my sponsor because every time I'm headed for the proverbial ditch, she just laughs and peers over her glasses and then totally and unerringly calls me on my crap. It is refreshing, sometimes painful, and exactly what I need to hear. I highly recommend working with a guide to explain this program, because in my experience, I could not and will not solve a problem with the same thinking that created it.

From a gift freely given, a simple program of spiritual work in which I engage on a daily basis, I have recovered from a hopeless state of mind and body. That's all I have, and it is enough for me. Thank you.

Dig Deep in One Place

Kim—Second Time Around

When I met Bill for the second time, I was full of despair, intolerable emptiness, shame, and self-loathing. Bill said, "I've been waiting for you and hoping you'd make it back." I had met Bill years earlier when I first came into a Twelve Step fellowship, and he was my sponsor. But through no fault of his, it didn't stick. I just wasn't ready for what recovery had to offer. The second time, however, it was different. I had nearly committed suicide and was desperate for relief. Bill, as ever, passed out hope like candy from his pocket.

We met one-on-one every week for nine months while we worked the thirty-six spiritual principles together. Slowly over time the fears that controlled my life and kept me hostage began to diminish, and the former spiritually bankrupt shell of a man started to have faith. For the first time in my life I knew I was a part of something much greater than myself and I belonged. Bill had gently guided me along so I could find my way out of the darkness and into the light. Today I can offer comfort and a solution to those who suffer as horribly as I did. Bill saved my life in a very real sense, and in doing so, he has potentially saved the lives of countless others through my continued efforts with those who still suffer. My gratitude to God, Bill, and the fellowship knows no bounds.

Eric—How Bill Changed my Life

Walking into a meeting at the fellowship club in the mountains of Colorado, I was struck by a couple of things. First, it sure enough was a "biker club," as I had been told; the place was full of black leather and black t-shirts. But I also saw that nearly all of these bikers carried a copy of the *Big Book*. These were both new experiences

For years, I had been in and out of the fellowship, not quite believing, not quite wanting to quit for good and all, and not quite ever having followed the clear-cut directions in the fellowship's basic text. But by July of 1995, all the not-quites were gone. I couldn't quit drinking for long, though I now wanted to, and I couldn't imagine life either with or without alcohol—a pretty bad place to be. A trigger-happy place to be.

Having read the book some and having had some persistent help from some recovered folks back in Texas who had found a solution to their problem, I knew that my only hope was that the Twelve Steps would work for me. I didn't believe they would, but I was desperate enough to be open to the idea. I knew also that my half-hearted measures of the past wouldn't be sufficient to solve my problem.

Bill was at that first fellowship club meeting and the one the next day where I approached him and asked him to help me. He spoke about his experience with the steps described in the book in his hand. It sounds almost trite, but I really do believe he had twinkling blue eyes that smiled easily and saw clear through my misery to the helpless soul within. "I'm on Step Four," I told him and then he asked, "So when was your last drink?" When I answered, "Tuesday," he suggested that we might want to back up a bit and start at the beginning. And so we did.

We met every Thursday there at the club following the 6:00 p.m. meeting. Bill would give me a reading assignment and then we would meet and he would read me that assignment—the whole thing. It wasn't very long before I realized that this technique of Bill reading me the book was very powerful. While I (the overeducated, multiple degree, well-read I) had read it just a few hours before, it seemed to come alive as Bill read it. The effect was amazing.

In about ten weeks we arrived at Step Ten, and I had my very own spiritual experience right there in a back room of the club. I quite suddenly realized that my great obsession was gone—gone!—and that I knew that not only did God exist, but that he existed within me. Within me—the last place I would have ever looked.

In the nearly seventeen years since that experience with Bill, I have taken something like five hundred other hopeless drunks or dope-fiends through that book, just as Bill did with me. It lands on some, plants a seed in others, and sends still others running away, but this work has entirely changed my whole attitude and outlook upon life. The wreckage from twenty years of indulgence has long ago been cleared up, and I am once again of real use to other people. I live in the conscious awareness of a Living Creator and I am a free man. All this and more just by following and continuing to follow "a few simple directions."

Bill's willingness to pass along to me what he had himself experienced saved my life first, but it changed it so irrevocably for the better that I can never fully repay such a debt. How *do* you repay a man for saving your life? Bill said, "Well you just pass it on —and don't miss out!" And so I do. And so I will.

Dusty—Seeing the Gift

I have an incredibly blessed life. I am happily married, have healthy children, am a successful entrepreneur, and have more friends than anyone could dream of, *and* I've had issues with alcohol, drugs, depression, loneliness, and desperation. My normal reaction to fear or disappointment was to turn on myself, which could be the source of great pain. I've read many books, seen doctors, and taken medications, all of which had the goal of "fixing" what was wrong and coincidentally involved very little action on my part.

Not so with Bill and Sandy.

They did not promise that in the blink of an eye, I'd transform my existence into an idyllic frolic free from all of life's conflicts. Instead, what they offered was a way of life *based in solution* . . . and here's the important piece: a detailed way to get and stay there!

Launching into my work with Bill and Sandy, there were times of anguish and an overwhelming sense that I might never be free from the past and my habitual fear. Inevitably and more often, though, I've been surprised by grace, strength, and the ability to forgive myself and others. Their remarkable insights and clarity assist in holding me steadfastly to the very freedom and happiness I've always dreamed of.

With Bill and Sandy's loving and honest guidance, I've been granted a confidence to implement personal solutions into my life on a daily basis as a woman who is strong, helpful, and human. Today, life is full of excitement, trust, and wonder as I've been trained well in the art of "seeing the gift" in all that it offers.

I will eternally bless them with my gratitude and love.

AFTERWORD

A Practical, Spiritual Life

Today our lives are rich and full. Most every morning we meet with people one on one guiding them through the Twelve Steps. Each meeting is about an hour long and focuses on one Step at a time. We do the same in the late afternoon, with work on our wood and glass projects and teaching through the day. The phone rings between twenty and forty times a day, and about half our weekends are devoted to speaking engagements and service opportunities in the fellowship. All this action keeps our focus on the Spiritual Principles, the only thing that keeps the progressive nature of fear out of our lives. We realize that spiritually we haven't arrived anywhere. We have only just begun.

We have discovered that if we will pursue the spiritual life, everything we need will come. This has been proved again and again in our daily lives over our years of recovery. The spiritual life is very easy, if we will be the gift instead of the problem. This is a spiritual life. It's a process of letting go of all the negative ideas that have held us back for so many years. Every day we start with a prayer for our bodies (exercise) and then a prayer with a little meditation. We read from spiritual literature and eat a healthy breakfast. Throughout the day we talk to others in recovery, go to a fellowship meeting, and find some way to be of help. There's nothing to it! We are prepared to help any human being on the face of the earth. We are talking about real help, not jobs, food, clothing, money, shelter, a date, or a new truck, but a way to overcome any difficulty that enters their lives. We know that this solution cannot be forced on anyone, but we will help anyone who reaches out to us. Anyone who is willing to do what is asked is never turned away.

We cherish our time alone together. Sometimes we just sit and read, but usually we talk and talk and talk. Sandy's mother once asked, what could we possibly still have to say to each other since you have been together all time? As our marriage and partnership deepen and grow, we find each other new and exciting. More and more it's a joy to have such a remarkable mate to share this journey. We write, cook, create, workout, and walk together. We know that everything is okay, no matter what anyone else says or does. Whether they accept our guidance or not, they will all reach home eventually.

If you get a chance, come by and see us. We would love to meet you. Remember, God's will for you is to be God. We are all in training to be angels. Put all the noise aside and be the gift. You are wonderful.

God bless you. We love you.

—Sandy and Bill

GRATITUDE

We wish to express our gratitude to all those who have taken the time to help us in the writing of this book. Your enthusiasm and love have kept us going when the project seemed overwhelming. You have all helped us to see the infinite possibilities of this universe.

To Dusty Meehan for your trust, love, encouragement, honest criticism, and suggestions, especially when it was difficult to do.

To Kristen Moeller—your adventures in writing challenged us to discover what was holding us back. Thank you for your willingness to share your experience with us.

To Layla Meehan for her wonderful photo of us today.

To Bill Thach, whose photo session with us so long ago produced the iconic portrait, "Bill and Sandy 1968."

To Rob, Kelly, Marya, Diana, Kim, Eric, and Dusty. Thank you for sharing your stories of recovery. You are all living examples of how the Twelve Steps can work in real life.

To all of you who read and helped to edit our early efforts at writing this book, your suggestions and comments all helped to shape this final product.

To all our old friends from Denver, Conifer, Bailey, and all over Colorado who all played a part in the drama. Thank you for participating and playing your roles so well.

We are filled with gratitude for those brave friends and family who participated in the 1992 intervention—Betty Deering, April

Montgomery, Kim Hartsen, Dwayne Taylor, Bruce MacMillan, and Michael Berry. Despite your fears, you started this incredible journey of recovery for us. Thank you

To the staff at Harmony Foundation—you planted the seeds that changed our lives. Howie, Martha, and Charlotte, to name only three, were instrumental in the process of discovery.

To all the folks who were there at our local Twelve Step club when we arrived to continue this journey. Your presence and participation over the years have been invaluable to this great adventure.

A special expression of gratitude to the all the people who have trusted us to guide them through the Twelve Steps. The gifts you have given us are priceless.

To our families who witnessed the insanity of our life and stayed the course, our gratitude knows no limits.

RESOURCES

Below is a list of fifty-three groups using the Twelve Steps as a basis for their programs. You can either contact one of these groups or start one of your own. The ways in which the Steps can be used are limitless.

AA	Alcoholics Anonymous	www.aa.org
AAA	All Addictions Anonymous	www.alladdictionsanonymous.org
ABA	Anorexics and Bulimics Anonymous	www.anorexicsandbulimicsanonymousaba.com
ACA	Adult Children of Alcoholics	www.adultchildren.org
Alanon/Alateen	For friends & family of Alcoholics	www.al-anon.alateen.org
ARTS	Arists Anonymous	www.artsanonymous.org
BA	Bettors Anonymous	www.bettorsanonymous.org
CA	Cocaine Anonymous	www.ca.org
CASA	Cleptomaniacs &Shoplifters Anonymous	www.kleptomanicsanonymous.com
CDA	Chemically Dependent Anonymous	www.cwaweb.org
CLA	Clutterers Anonymous	www.clutterersanonymous.org
CMA	Crystal Meth Anonymous	www.crystalmeth.org

Co-Anon	For friends & family of cocaine addicts	www.co-anon.org
CoDA	Co-Dependents Anonymous	www.codependents.org
COSA	Codependents of Sex Addicts	www.cosa-recovery.org
COSLAA	CoSex and Love Addicts Anonymous	www.coslaa.org
DA	Debtors Anonymous	www.debtorsanonymous.org
DRA	Dual Diagnoses/ Recoveries Anonymous	www.draonline.org
EA	Emotions Anonymous	www.emotionsanonymous.org
EAA	Eating Addictions Anonymous	www.eatingaddictionsanonymous.org
EDA	Eating Disorders Anonymous	www.eatingdisordersanonymous.org
EHA	Emotional Health Anonymous	www.flash.net/~sgveha
FA	Families Anonymous	www.familiesanonymous.org
FA	Food Addicts in Recovery Anonymous	www.foodaddicts.org
FAA	Food Addicts Anonymous	www.foodaddictsanonymous.org
GA	Gamblers Anonymous	www.gamblersanonymous.org

Gam-Anon	For friends & families of problem gamblers	www.gam-anon.org
HCV	Hepatitus Anonymous	www.hcvanonymous.org
HIV AIDS	HIV AIDS Anonynous	www.hivanonymous.org
IDAA	International Doctors in AA	www.idaa.org
ILAA	International Lawyers in AA	www.ilaa.org
LAA	Love Addicts Anonymous	www.loveaddicts.org
MA	Marijuana Anonymous	www.marijuana-anonymous.org
NA	Narcotics Anonymous	www.na.org
NAIL	Neurotics Anonymous	www.neuroticosanonimosusa.org
Nar-Anon	For families and friends of addicts	www.nar-anon.org
NicA	Nicotine Anonymous	www.nicotineanonymous.org
OA	Overeaters Anonymous	www.oa.org
OCA	Obsessive Compulsive Anonymous	www. obsessivecompulsiveanonymous.org
OLGA	Online Gamblers Anonymous	www.olga.org
P.A.	Procastinators Anonymous	www.procrastinators-anonymous.org

PA	Pills Anonymous	www.pillsanonymous.org
PA	Parents Anonymous	www.parentsanonymous.org
RA	Recoveries Anonymous	www.r-a.org
RCA	Recovering Couples Anonymous	www.recovering-couples.org
SA	Sexaholics Anonymous	www.sa.org
SA	Spenders Anonymous	www.spenders.org
SAA	Sex Addicts Anonymous	www.sexaa.org
SCA	Sexual Compulsives Anonymous	www.sca-recovery.org
SIA	Survivors of Incest Anonymous	www.siawsa.org
SMA	Self Mutilators Anonymous	www.sclfmutilatorsanonymous.org
TA	Post Traumatic Stress Anonymous	www.ptsdanonymous.org
WA	Workaholics Anonymous	www.workaholics-anonymous.org

AUTHOR BIO

Since 1965 Bill and Sandy Fifield have worked in partnership to perfect their artistic passions in wood and glass. The intricacy of Sandy's stained, beveled and fused glass is facilitated by her background as a maker of fine jewelry. Bill is an artist, designer and craftsman who uses master woodworking techniques and folk art methods to make everything from entry doors, desks, tables and chairs to hand-carved gun cases, mantles, pillars, corbels, and Adirondack twig furniture.

In mid-1992 when recovery entered their lives, they enthusiastically threw themselves into helping others. In the following nineteen years, they have never been without a volunteer position. In conjunction with service, they have mentored over 1500 people on a one-to-one basis. Based on the Alcoholics Anonymous Twelve Step program of recovery, mentoring experience and commitment to "passing it on," they have developed into dynamic, popular and engaging speakers. Their workshops draw from their own first-hand knowledge of the challenges and importance of a structured, guided and simple path to personal accountability. The Fifields have traveled primarily throughout the southwest speaking to groups ranging from ten to eight hundred.

When they're not out being of service to others, Bill and Sandy are likely making art (and a mess) in their studio, writing, teaching students or walking their beloved Scottie dog, Thistle, on their beautiful mountain property in Conifer, Colorado 35 miles SW of Denver. They also enjoy vigorously working out and dishing out enormous amounts of gratitude to everyone they see. They have truly dug deep in one place.

CPSIA information can be obtained at www.ICGtesting.com
Printed in the USA
LVOW13s0320030314

375788LV00002B/135/P